GRANDMOTHER DREAMS

CONVERSATIONS ACROSS THE VEIL

Jennifer Shoals

For Connie —
we are the journey
of our spirits walking
the earth

BALBOA
PRESS

A DIVISION OF HAY HOUSE

ISBN: 978-1-4525-5301-6 (sc)
ISBN: 978-1-4525-5302-3 (e)
ISBN: 978-1-4525-5303-0 (hc)

Library of Congress Control Number: 2012909582

Balboa Press books may be ordered through booksellers or by contacting:

Balboa Press
A Division of Hay House
1663 Liberty Drive
Bloomington, IN 47403
www.balboapress.com
1-(877) 407-4847

Because of the dynamic nature of the Internet, any web addresses or links contained in this book may have changed since publication and may no longer be valid. The views expressed in this work are solely those of the author and do not necessarily reflect the views of the publisher, and the publisher hereby disclaims any responsibility for them.

The author of this book does not dispense medical advice or prescribe the use of any technique as a form of treatment for physical, emotional, or medical problems without the advice of a physician, either directly or indirectly. The intent of the author is only to offer information of a general nature to help you in your quest for emotional and spiritual well-being. In the event you use any of the information in this book for yourself, which is your constitutional right, the author and the publisher assume no responsibility for your actions.

Cover art: Jennifer Shoals with Maryl Skinner and Denny FitzPatrick of M Graphic Design (mgraphic@boreal.org)

Printed in the United States of America

Balboa Press rev. date: 06/25/2012

For Clay and Lily and all the world's children,
whose future is being created by the choices we make now.

Contents

Introduction

We exist in many worlds. These worlds, both seen and unseen, are layers of energy that spread around us in concentric spheres.

The layer most obvious to our senses is our physical body. Formed at conception and disintegrating with death, the body provides a home during the lifetime of our physical journey. For each of us, our physical form is the center of our existence.

Energy layers ripple outward from this physical center as we interact with the environment. We breathe in, breathe out, eat, eliminate. The energy in our bodies and in nature is in constant contact, being shared and transformed. We are made up of each other.

The energy layers of physical reality continue to spread outward as our being interacts with our neighbors—plants, animals, and other humans. Our personal energy is also part of the energy that makes up families and communities, as well as political and geographic concentrations. We are also energy members of planet Earth, the solar system, the Milky Way, and eventually the Infinite Universe. These worlds are not separate. They are contained in each other and present simultaneously at every moment. We may not be constantly aware of all these layers, but they are always present and our energy is included in theirs.

We also extend in energy layers in the other direction—inward. Inside our bodies, we know that we are made up of body systems: Our lungs breathe. Our blood is pumped and filtered. Nerves fire. Chemicals are produced and released. Multiple body systems all work together every second of every day around the clock to maintain our physical survival. When we look closer, we can see that every one of those body systems is made up of cells. The cells are made of cell components, which are made of molecules, which are made of atoms, and atomic particles and on and on. Just like our outer universe, our inner universe stretches farther than our ability to see, measure, or comprehend.

All of these layers and all of these worlds are connected through a mysterious energy which we call Life Force.

There are even more layers in motion beyond our usual awareness. This physical body, for example—this great gift which is A Center of the Universe, where does it come from? Every one of us is the product of the joining of an egg and a sperm. Each egg and sperm is a single-celled carrier of genetic material. Genetic chemical coding is nature's computer program—it carries all of the information needed to create an incredibly complex human being. Where does this coded program come from? It comes from our ancestors—our parents, our grandparents, and their great-great-grandparents. We are generally aware of three to four generations back in time, but there have already been at least *a hundred thousand* generations of recognizable humans. Ultimately, this family tree unites you and me and everyone through the same ancestors from millions of years ago. We really are all related. It's not just some cute cliché. It is a fact. The human family tree spreads out from its roots like a giant net, and every one of us is in it.

Within this relatedness, there is also diversity. Each egg and each sperm are unique. There are no two exactly the same, and when one of each joins the other, a novel mix is created. Some inherited traits are obvious. I may have my father's ears, or my grandmother's eyes. But I just might have some cells in my right arm from a Mongolian hunter or some cells in my left leg from a Peruvian mountain runner. Bits of the gray matter in my brain may be from an African bush woman of fifty thousand years ago. I *have* lived other lives. Not me personally, but parts of the present me have existed all through history and some of them are now expressed in my current body. All of those parts of me also had experiences during their existence, and information from those historical experiences has been transferred to my body, in my cells, through DNA. This transferred effect is what is being looked at in the current study of epigenetics.

One of the functions of DNA is to carry information forward. Every time a human is born, they do not start out as a Neanderthal. We have the benefit of our ancestors, who developed ways to adapt and survive with each passing generation. Those adaptations created biological impressions. What if we could access those impressions, the stored information of past lives and experiences in our DNA, the wisdom in our cellular memory? If we could hear that rich history, stories and universal truths would appear. It would be worth listening.

Using meditative energy practice, I have developed a way of being that allows me to access this information. When I clear my mind and ask a question without bias, information surfaces. Somewhat like the old eight-ball fortune-telling toy, the answer floats up into my consciousness. If I choose to accept the answer, no matter how far-fetched or incomprehensible it seems, then I may continue with the conversation. I can ask more unbiased questions and receive more information. When I express doubt or attempt to answer from my own ego's needs, the conversation fades. I have learned to put a great deal of trust in these conversations. Because the information presented is often well beyond my own level of development, I know that it is coming from somewhere beyond my normal consciousness. This not an intellectual process that occurs in my brain. This is an intuitive process. It comes through my body. Information is collected in my spine and then translated through my mind. I originally called these interactions 'Conversations with the Universe'. Eventually, I realized that this information came from Universal Wisdom, which is also known as the Collective Unconscious—the infinite pool of wisdom created by and available to all beings.

I have had conversations with Universal Wisdom for many years. I used this access primarily to help me with my personal life, navigating many crises and healing deep trauma with this wealth of objective guidance. On an autumn day in 2005, I went on a strenuous hike through rugged terrain. As usual, I spent the first few miles striding through my everyday concerns, and then I fell into a comfortable state of walking meditation. Around mile seven I became aware that another presence from the dream world—the world beyond our five senses, was traveling with me. As I walked, this presence gave me the directive to start this book. Although I experienced some fear and did not understand what the book would be about, I committed faithfully to the task. The title *Grandmother Dreams* was given to me first, and then the writing project began.

Over the next three years I deepened my meditative conversations. In the beginning, the process required a step-by-step ritual of grounding and thanksgiving in order to reach the dream world. Over time I developed daily energy habits that allowed instant access in any moment. Most days now, the "real" world (the physical world of the five senses) and the dream world (the world beyond the five senses) are intertwined. This book was written as I simultaneously traveled in the Dream World and typed on a laptop. It is a series of channeled interviews—question and answer sessions distilled from hundreds of interactive conversations.

My very first contacts in the dream world occurred a decade before that autumn walk with a woman who had been known to me in the physical world—my mother's mother. I was in the midst of healing a childhood rape when my grandmother appeared in a guided dream and offered me much-needed support. That contact eventually expanded to a group of elder women I know as "the Grandmothers." They are wise, patient, supportive, and always available. Over time, my dream world contacts have grown to include many elders, female and male, as well as spiritual guides of all ages and cultural origin.[1] Their names appear in bold at the beginning of each conversation. As I interviewed them, these contacts taught me how to place my being in a meditative zone where it is possible to communicate "across the

---

1   This book presents the voices of a variety of people from different cultures, age groups, genders, and historical times. I am not speaking for or representing any of these groups. They speak and I record their words. Our intention is to foster understanding.

veil." Teachers from the other side either travel to me or I to them, in order to transmit specific information and knowledge.

Unlike Universal Wisdom, which is generalized information from the pool of all beings, each Teacher comes through specific memories carried in my cells. Each Teacher is an individual with a personality. They sometimes express feelings like anger or humor, and interaction with them demands patience and attention to their needs. Being invited by a Teacher to enter the Great Unknowing may take several forms. I may be offered entrance through an open window with white mist on the other side, a Teacher may swallow me into their body, or I may swallow them into my body.

It benefits me personally to travel in this way—I gain much knowledge and always return refreshed. The Teachers have told me, however, that this information is intended to be heard by many. According to these Teachers, it is time now for humans to realize and accept that which is beyond the perceived physical realm—to expand across the veil. It is time for humans to evolve into another layer of conscious reality. Access to this expanded reality requires creating a home for Spirit within our being, moving our attention away from time in favor of space, and placing our Ego in service to Spirit. This shift is not just an internal process. It also includes taking action, action with the purpose of moving Spirit and embodying Love, of experiencing and expressing Compassion.

The title *Grandmother Dreams* describes both the vehicle and the process through which this desired shift in human experience is to occur. The stories passed down through cellular memory and Universal Wisdom are the dreams of the 'Grandmothers'—of our ancestors. The shift we experience when we learn to expand beyond the five senses is a kind of waking dream. Because we are the grandmothers and grandfathers of tomorrow, when we choose to make this shift we will be actively dreaming human experience into the next evolutionary level of development.

We Are Always in The Presence

My **Grandmother Martha** was a strong woman who lived ninety-seven years. She passed on in the year 2000. She told me the following story in 2007:

There is a story I would like to tell about when I was little. There was a man who lived down the road, when we were on the farm. He used to sell milk in these big cans. The milk was beautiful and fresh. We liked to eat the cream off the top. I don't know if I can tell this. Well, he had a daughter. She used to help with those big cows, even though she was quite small. She had short blond hair. One time, she was sitting on a stool, and one of those cows kicked, and she got it right in the side of the head. It was right on the ear, and it pushed in the side of her head. She fell down, and lay there in the straw with her eye bulging out and staring. I wanted her to get up and walk, even with that eye bulging. I pulled on her arm. I was screaming at her to get up, get up, and I was pulling on her arm. Her shoulder was jerking up and down with my pulling. Her daddy came in and took her hand out of mine and put her arm down on her side. He put his arm around me. I was crying. I was only seven or eight. He kneeled down with his arm around me and talked softly, comforting me. He said how Lornie was going to be resting now, and I should take some cream over to my mother's house. He filled up a little can, and I walked down the road with it. I think I would have had nightmares my whole life about that girl and the bulging eye. But here that man was so kind to me while his little daughter lay there dead. How could he be like that? I have thought about that so many times, and all I can say is that there are moments when you know God is there.

You have to believe that God is always here.
All you need to do is be open.

It is important to acknowledge that using the word "God" may be uncomfortable for some of us. **Universal Wisdom** helped me to understand why the word is important and why it is given preference in these writings:
You are uncomfortable using the word God.
It has so much political baggage and judgment attached to it.
That is you, not the word. You need to become more comfortable with the word. Yes, because you will need to use it and you can't be squeamish with it. It is a word that Westerners understand deep in their psyche—it refers to a deeper place. New Age terms will deflect some of the meaning from it. There is no substitute at this point.

Martha said, "All you need to do is be open." This book will address the need to be open and ways to create that opening. What we need to be open *to* is directly related to our purpose in life. According to **Universal Wisdom**, our purpose revolves around the expression of Love, the process of energy transfer that occurs in situations like the exchange between Lornie's father and Little Martha.[2]
It would be a good time to talk about Love. Love is the backbone of this experience on earth. Your purpose is to manifest God's Pure Love on earth. Love is important because it is a renewable energy. There is no limit to the generation of it.

---

2   There is a difference between *love* and *Love*. Lower-case-L love is a sentimental, conditional state which we refer to when we say "I love baseball" or "I love chocolate." Capital-L Love describes a state of spiritual connection. It is the kind of Love that Mother Teresa expressed—inclusive, compassionate and unconditional.

During my childbearing years I became aware that each time a baby is born, there is more Love made, more than existed before that.
Exactly.

I am sensing a connection between Love and the spaciousness that occurs when I am Touched By God. ("Touched By God" refers to a body-psyche sensation that occurs when I am completely in the present moment and connected to Divine Radiance. It is both totally overwhelming and totally freeing.)

They are not the same thing. Being Touched By God is a state of openness and expansion, which allows Love energy to enter into deeper places. The receptors for this energy are everywhere, but humans so often have their energy misaligned, not centered, so there is not a stable foundation for supporting more energy.

I feel that when I am overtired.

That is one block, so much energy being used for survival. And the other block is being on a high, Ego filling and filling and demanding more. There needs to be a balance, rest and flow. And it all needs to be balanced among the body centers.

How does that work for people with chronic or terminal illness?

People with chronic illness have to find another alignment. This is a different topic.

Terminal illness actually allows the window to open further, as the body's physical needs drop away. There is a greater capacity to be Touched by God, but less ability to move that toward others. The opportunity in dying is that the people who witness this have an opportunity to open. There are many opportunities, every day. Every minute.

One barrier that exists is the human belief system that Love has to be earned, that somehow people have to deserve it. That implies a limited supply, which is false. The Love is there, one only has to be open to it.

My rational mind is stuck here. I can believe that Love is endless, and then I also wonder where it comes from, and if there is currently this outside push to increase Love consciousness then doesn't that imply an impending shortage?

Love is a manifestation of Life Force. You see Life Force all around you, in the bursting forth of green summer. Love is a higher vibration, a higher harmonic. All of the harmonics are important—they work together. The human harmonic of Love is distinct and necessary. Yes, you are right, there are so many humans now, you would think that there would be much Love. But humans are losing sight of their original purpose. It is important that our memories of Original Love, of Life Force, hum up. Because this is what humans are here for and what will ultimately save you.

I'm nervous about entering into a fear-factor arena with this—spreading intimidation through the claim that there is going to be a big die-off, and we have to prepare to save ourselves from extinction. This is so prevalent in society now and it is driving a lot of the ego imbalance.

This is true. Humans are sensing the coming shifts and don't understand what they are feeling, so it is channeled into fear. One of the ego's jobs is to preserve bodily life, survival. In the face of this vague sense of fear, ego is accelerating.

It's like an addiction. Ego has gotten us into this position of disharmony, and then the danger of the situation stimulates even more ego response.

An imbalance. That is why it is important to create more opportunities for Spirit. It is important to bring Love into the physical realm. Manifesting Love creates a physical resonance, creating realignment.

The flower children of the '60s got sidetracked into Love as sex.

Sexual union is a place where Spirit can manifest. That requires emotional intimacy. Few have the courage to practice this.

To be emotionally naked and unashamed.

Yes.

Please discuss harmonics in relation to Love.

Resonance. Vibration. Harmony means that they balance into a larger tone.

Looking in the dictionary turns out to be helpful. The dictionary describes harmonics as a fundamental vibration that, when energized, can influence other vibrations. An energy example would be sound. When one string on a musical instrument is lightly touched, the strings on either side of it will also vibrate at a related frequency. Overtones are created.

When a person becomes more aligned with Love, the frequency of their energy also touches the energy of those around them. This harmonious vibration of energy resonates with others and the sum effect is a "humming up," an increase in overall Love energy. This occurred when Lornie's father showed loving compassion for Martha. Not only was her distress soothed by his energy, but she was moved to consider compassion herself. The energy vibration of his action added harmony to the world through Love.

This is our true purpose in life.

There is power in relationships. Obviously, it's the basis of Love—transference.

The basis is personal, individual. It's about what happens when someone opens themselves to the vibration of Love. That changes the vibration in the cells, cellular energy. In the state of True Love people are able to make cleaner connections with others. The vibrations occur in a person, and the person who is opened is then able to move energy in others, which assists them in opening also. Feeling the vibration gives another the opportunity to choose to open.

I'm thinking about the spaciousness of opening, how I feel like there is beautiful space between every cell in my body, and there is a tranquility associated with that.

It is the calming effect of returning to original state, unconfined by the physical body. Expansiveness is original state.

Is this who Star Sky Forever is?[3]

Star Sky Forever is a way of seeing yourself in your original state.

I need to bring that forth, express it, not keep it inside.

That would be part of your opening.

---

3   Star Sky Forever is a personal name given to the universal me that is beyond Ego. I met this part of myself when I made a pilgrimage to Wounded Knee in South Dakota. Weeping at the cemetery, my white-skinned outer body asked forgiveness from the brown-skinned who had been murdered there. My white skin peeled back to reveal Brown Being, a brown layer underneath, my connection to all our ancestors. At the moment my brown-skinned self granted compassionate forgiveness for the unforgivable, the brown layer peeled back to reveal the entire Universe inside me, the One With All. I appeared as the infinite night sky full of stars, and I was given the name Star Sky Forever. When I feel judgmental about someone, I ask myself, "Could that person be a star in my sky?" Because the stars are infinite, the answer is always "yes."

I'm also thinking about the "wisdom of unknowing." Is that what is in the space?

It's part of it. Unknowing is the moment when ego control (personality) is given up. It is the invitation to be Touched By God.

I have been practicing "not needing to know," giving up the need to constantly make decisions about things that have not happened yet. It frees me up to be much more in the present, and to meet each event as it unfolds instead of predetermining how it is going to be.

Allowing the present is necessary to be Touched By God. Love occurs in the present. The moment is all there is.

And it is so fleeting.

It is not something to hold on to or attain. It is being. Being unfolds. Controlling folds up. Unfolding is what life is doing. Even in death and decay, there is unfolding. Unfolding is Life Force.

The new green sprouts, reaching.

Life Force.

Mamas rocking their babies.

Life Force.

Opening to Love requires that we go back to our original self, connected to God. Our Ego is the part of us that maintains survival. It is our personality, our "me first". Living primarily through Ego creates barriers that block our return to God, our original self. If we are going to be open to Love, then we need to give up the control that our Ego craves. We do not have to denounce Ego, to get rid of it, as many spiritual leaders today recommend. We need to acknowledge it as part of the whole and then step into the larger space that is our original self.

During one conversation, I kept hearing the word "judge." The dictionary has four entries in noun form: high-ranking court official, adjudicator (appointed to assess), someone giving an opinion, Jewish warrior/leader. There were six entries for the verb form: to act as a judge, to adjudicate, to assess, to consider or reckon, to estimate, to condemn.

I usually think of judgment as "condemn." It's more basic meaning is about determining relative value. "Judge not" could mean "don't condemn," which is a pretty narrow interpretation, or it could mean "don't place a value on." Placing value is a hierarchical activity, which implies "more than" or "less than," superior or inferior. In Buddhist thought, knowing renders the mind static. Not knowing makes room. Know, not-know. Judge, judge-not—I feel that I am off on a semantics sidebar.

Universal Wisdom: *You're not.*

Where does this go?

Back to Love.

Mother Teresa said that if we judge people, then we will have no time to love them.

Yes.

So I am to work on judgment?

No.

Meet a judge?

Yes.

I feel so tired. Like I could fall into sleep.

That is trance state.

Stop thinking.

Yes.

(Pause.)

Go ahead.

[Now the information is coming in a man's voice, booming deep and stern.

He is **The Judge**.

Go ahead. I will be the stenographer. What is the lesson today?

The lesson is "genuine".

I think that I don't respond or question, is that correct?

Mostly. You have to make way.

Really get my ego out of it. Drop that. Zero my agenda. I am breathing into hara, my center .

Being genuine does not mean being who you think you really are. Genuine is about going back to Original Self. Self before it detached from center. Back into the seed of Being. Back into the wisdom energy

7

of that seed. Many people believe that meditation/prayer is what we use to go beyond ourselves. But really, what we need to do is go back to our genuine self. The One With All.

When we are One With All, then we have dissolved the boundaries that divide one thing from another, pushing back away from ego. We do not have to denounce ego. We can accept that it exists, part of the All. And we can choose, at the same time, to move down into the genuine self, the seed. The seed holds everything. We are all of the same seed. The seed is the starting point, a tiny hole, and when we pass through it we will be the entire universe.

I want to tell you another thing. This is something you cannot understand, but you must write it anyway. It may be needed later. You must write that when the story reigns, all will be destroyed. The story is very powerful. The story can be held back by children laughing. It is the only way to save the planet—children laughing. Be kind to those who cannot laugh. Bring help to those who weep. Shun sympathy. Live. Don't think that you are immortal. Don't live by yourself. Live by others. Help them.

Judge not.

Judge not.

"If we are to have real peace, we must begin with the children."
—Mahatma Gandhi

The Judge spoke to me again at a later date:

There is nothing you can do to save yourself. There is only one way—connect with what is right and follow that. It is a sensation. A sense of going toward what is right. It is a gut sensation. That is the collective rhythm of the cells, the vibration of harmony. When you move beyond your ego, then you will be able to sense this vibration. It strengthens when the path is true. The more you listen to it, the better you are able to hear it. Following this sensation leads you to a better life. People call it gut instinct. That is part of it, intuition. But it also involves a resonance with cellular memory.

We are given a code to live by. It is the code that underlies not only survival and evolution, but purpose. Wild animals know this code. Humans can be aware of it. But many factors in our environment can dull awareness. People want this awareness, but have lost the ability to listen for it and feed it. Much of American culture invites humans to forget this vibration, to cover it up with dull lifestyle—focusing on being busy, accomplishing tasks, overeating, eating poorly, not moving around, staying indoors, fleeing emotions, attempting to cover up the vibration because it does not appear to mesh with the modern world. Then people function in a disconnected state, and decisions are made which ensure further disconnection. Look at how easily we kill. War is a disconnect. Violence is a disconnect. Drugs are a disconnect. Any addiction is a disconnect. What we are disconnected from is Purpose. People want to have a reason to be. It is all easy. It can be felt. But only if we listen for the vibration of the cells.

That is the force that drives Life.

Yes. It is visible everywhere. Growth of plants and animals is the most obvious. And relationships. Not romance, but Love. The love of a parent for a child, when it is clean and unconditional. Everyone wants this, because that is where you feel alive. It makes the cells vibrate in harmony.

Then why would people avoid it?

Because it can be very powerful. Some are afraid of it, of that feeling of power, because they have been trained to avoid it.

I assume people can train themselves to be unafraid of it.

They must be trained, or at least come to an awareness of it. There is too little to sustain the planet, like a dying language.

So it is not just a problem in America or the West?

No. But that is where the biggest void is, and that is where the biggest change can be made, the biggest effect. American culture has a great influence around the world. Currently, that influence is destructive.

But it seems that the reason there is so much influence is because of advertising, which is a major supporter of the disconnect—don't feel, just buy more stuff. A channel is already there, and it is full of negativity.

That is partly true. A channel is there, an opening has been made. But this change will not be disseminated through commercialism. It is a person-to-person channel. Direct contact has to be made. Human contacts need to be reestablished. Like stones in a pond, there will be ripple effects.

Then why am I writing a book? That seems like indirect contact.
But moving the book around will make contact occur.
It's not the book—it's discussing the contents.
Yes.
Because that contact will stimulate the vibrations.
Yes.
So, while I am focused on the book, and the stories, I also need to be cultivating understanding of the vibrations and their transmission.
Start with the vibrations. What kind of vibration is stirred by any story?
Somehow tied to emotion, to feeling.
Definitely.
There needs to be a capacity for feeling, for feeling feelings, for understanding them, for transferring them. Are we doing that now with anger?
The feeling is being stirred, but not learned from. It has the capacity to be transformative, but that is not now being utilized.
We have stagnated at the level of destruction?
Yes. Ultimately, what we want to foster is growth.
And we are stuck on growth of product, GNP, stuff.
Which is ultimately destructive, because it does not recognize limits.
And what we want to focus on is energy.
Positive energy.
Cultivating Life Force.
Yes.
What has happened to Christianity?
It should be focusing on doing good.
But many Christian people are stuck in their egos.
They are thinking, "I am good," when they need to focus on "this is good."
The "this" that is giving without strings attached. Mother Teresa giving.
Yes.
And how about people like me, who have been turned off by Christianity?
You need to make room for it. Being judgmental is not helpful. Everyone is trying, in some way or another. Not everyone is skillful.

The Judge asked us to focus on the vibration, the feeling of being in a connected state. The following conversation is a good example of working with a Teacher's personal style, but it also illuminates just what the sensation of universal Love feels like:

Pete is a Teacher I have met several times, and I think of him as For-Pete's-Sake. Pete is a goofy intellectual artist type with long, wavy gray hair. I smile when I think of him. It's kind of like he's doing a little stand-up comedy for me. He's somewhat irreverent, yet understands the Universal Wisdom channel completely. Who are you, Pete?

I'm your man.

The man I want to meet?

Of course.

I feel like you're playing with me.

I'd love to.

Are you a real person? Living now?

I think so.

This is going to be difficult—maybe these responses come with silly questions.

Yup.

(Note: I have come to understand that asking irrelevant questions leads to these short, unhelpful answers, whether I am speaking with a Teacher or Universal Wisdom. It is a clue that I am off track, following my own agenda, and need to let the speaker lead.)

So what would you tell me today?

I would tell you that all this stuff is very real, and lots of people are buying it.

I heard that *The Secret* was on *Oprah*.

It's spreading.

I have a sense that you are somewhere in publishing.

Could be.

What advice do you have for this writing project?

Get it done, then see me.

I am having a most pleasant sensation right now. Through my entire being, I feel relaxed and joyful, actually joyful. I am very present in my body, engulfed by expansive warmth and complete harmony. I am enjoying that. I feel like I'm in love.

That's what being in Love feels like.

I guess I imagined it as more neutral. I suppose I could only think of it as the absence of pain. It's actually a state of well-being. Well Being. Harmony. Balance.

Love.

So that is what Life Force is. No wonder plants want to reach for the sky and into the earth. No wonder children want to play and laugh. It's exuberant. This is the "feeling" that needs to be advanced. It's something that can only be mimicked, temporarily, by drugs or any other addiction. True well-being is internally generated—cellular harmony. Who wouldn't want to feel this way? It's freeing and expansive. Generous. Loving. Complete connection.

You are cultivating Life Force.

This wonderful feeling of Universal Love is something that people instinctively want to experience. It is the misdirected drive behind most of our addictions, and it is what we are seeking in our relationships. The following conversation with **Universal Wisdom** explores where we need to be in order to experience this kind of Love, and addresses our responsibility to create openings for this experience:

Why are relationships so hard?

Everybody's roles are changing. The ground keeps shifting.

It seems like the connection needs to be on some human-spirit level, but there is this sexual dynamic between women and men that keeps pulling in another direction.

There is biology, and there is psyche. They are related.

One is physical, and one is spiritual.

It is hard to find a balanced connecting point.

What about the effect of culture?
Culture influences brain patterns.
Like media, training the physical body to react to certain stimuli.
Those are feelings. Their chemical origin is in the brain.
And how does this word-meditation-conversation that we are doing work?
It is cellular, and the information is sent through the spine.
Not the brain, because of environmental conditioning?
Because of the intellect.
It clouds the info.
It filters it. This only works with unfiltered information.
How does the mind fit in this?
The mind is the bigger energy. Your spine is the amplifier, the focus. Your mind is everywhere.
Carlos Castaneda describes an egg-shaped human field that has a focal point, called the assemblage point, behind the shoulder—a point with energy filaments from the Universe passing through it.
It fits.
What is that point behind the shoulder that he talks about?
It is the focus field. Move your energy back into it to remember the bigger picture.
The mind.
And more.
What is the more?
Carlos described it as different states of attention. Some people call it the other worlds. It is beyond usual perception.
Beyond biology.
Yes. Beyond every construct anyone can imagine.
How is it that I am functioning in this state, sitting in my body and typing on a laptop while allowing the flow?
Because you are willing. It requires suspension of the physical mind while you're participating.
Yes, I see that. While I was asking the question, I became more aware of the keyboard, the click of typing, and now I feel pulled off into the physical world again.
Calling it states of attention is somewhat accurate.

13

I assume that the information flowing forth is coming from some ancestral memory. Is that true?
Somewhat.
There seems to be a difference between this kind of conversation and the one with a Teacher. One is more directed.
Yes.
Is any of it from outside?
Yes.
And inside at the same time?
Not always.
Some is just outside?
None of it is just outside.
Because the mind is everywhere.
Yes.
But why isn't my mind all tangled up with the minds of other people?
They are all the same.
So we all have this access.
The potential.
I haven't thought about Carlos Castaneda for a long time, but it is all flooding in here. He had contact with others who were sharing attentional space.
Yes.
This is a ways off for me.
Yes.
I am supposed to be focusing on the flow there is, practicing.
Yes.
That is what I have been missing about the discipline. It is practice so I can move deeper and further.
Yes.
But the information is also important.
Right now, it is the reason to do this. There is a critical time period now, when much information needs to be transmitted to as many as possible.
I need to be responsible. It makes me shudder. I already have so much responsibility.

That is all physical, except for connecting your children to spirit world. This is a different kind of responsibility. This is about the survival of Love.

The Life Force kind of Love.

Yes.

I have some notion that there is much work to do, and there is a deadline.

No one can wait.

So I need to think of another word besides responsibility. Management. Labor of Love. Filling with energy. Passion. Maybe passion is it. What is the Passion of Christ, anyway?

It's about making a sacrifice.

As a single parent and a health-care worker, this is a word I recoil from. More sacrifice. But there *is* something I am driven to do— make a difference. What else would I be here for? Just to suck up all the physical pleasures I can find? Then dry up to dust and blow away? It's something else. There is a purpose. To Love. To make more Love. Nurture it and make room. Sacrifice is more about making space, balancing this physical existence, balancing self with relationship, balancing spirit with body. So, the concept you are leading me into describes managing balance? Managing sounds so business-like. Balancing energy. Energy balancing.

You're on the right track.

How about Love movement.

Closer.

"Love" is so distracting, the whole trippy-hippie thing.

They were trying to get there, too.

And Love is the word I relate to.

It's not about words.

Words are intellect. I need an opening into the spine. Maybe I don't need to name it.

It needs a name to be recognized.

I just saw it with my mind's eye: "Love Memory."

That's it.

Because we have to go back to where we came from—the big soup, Life Force. Love.

Remember that Life Force is not static. It is moving, it is circular.
This reminds me of an experience I had with a Native Drum Circle. As the drums opened my psyche, I was shown a vision of the thread of life. The thread of life was coming full circle in a big hoop, beginning and ending at the same point. My current existence in time was a cocoon on the thread. Healing is about straightening the kinks in the loop, the healing going into the past and into the future, and the smoother the looping of the thread, the better the transmission of energy, of Love, of Life Force. Love Memory. That is what this is all about—pulling back all of the stray energy that is going into hate and judgment and war and destruction—and understanding our origin and our fate, threading a new destiny.
Oh, my. I see the work now. I see the path. I'm already on it.
It is big work.
It is beautiful work.
Yes.
Thank you so much for trusting me, for returning over and over to help me see.
Thank yourself for staying open.
And big thanks to Everything That Is, for making me able and willing to take this path, to have this life, to keep me believing, ever since the beginning. "This little light of mine, I'm gonna let it shine."
That is Love Memory, sustaining you.
I feel so filled right now. Humbled by gratefulness. How wise the world is! Big thanks.

While I was sleeping one night, a Teacher came to me in a dream. In the dream, I was visiting a farmhouse in Ireland. I had a pile of papers in my hands, small papers like receipts of all different sizes. I was trying to gather them up, but they were crumpled and jumbled and I was frustrated. A man came over and said not to worry. He said he would help me make sense of those papers. He had curly, reddish blond hair pulled back in a ponytail. He was gentle and kind. His name was **Ronnie Wall**, and he was going to help me put the interviews for this book in order.

A meditation interview with him occurred several weeks later. In that interview, Ronnie talked about the importance of Love in the universe, and went on to highlight the need for inclusiveness in the changes that we are to make—the importance of finding Common Ground and common spirit with others:

I see ground, earth. I see an Irish farm. I am back at the small farm house on rocky soil. The man with the curly red hair is sitting across the room, looking at me with an intriguing grin. Ronnie, do you still want to help me with my papers?

I've been waiting all of this time, haven't I? (He speaks with a very thick brogue.)

Yes, a long time. Weeks. I'm here now, ready to listen and write. Where do you want to start?

It's this writin' project of yours.

Yes, this project. It is a jumble of papers. You know something about that.

I suppose.

I will be quiet again and listen.

Yes, there can't be interruptin'.

It's a fine line between madness and spiritual enlightenment. Frightening, it can be. That's why so many afear it. Afraid that they wouldn't come back if they went there. Using daily life to numb it out, rather than face it. We are all right there. Right in the hand of God. Just choose not to see it. Frightening, it is. Because it's the same face we come from and we'll go back to when it's our time. We're afraid of that face because it is so powerful. It is the whole everything at once. It's beyond our ability to understand in human life form. Our bodies are made up of it, and that's mostly unconscious. When we're not in a physical form, we can tolerate more, because we don't have such boundaries to maintain. It's a lot of work keepin' a body going. It takes energy. That's one of the reasons we get so tired. We're focusin' always on that task. It would help a person to set some guidelines for living and then let that take care of itself. Let your energy get on top of that. Not so you forget it or don't enjoy it. Oh,

17

no. One of the gifts of this body is the pleasure it can bring. Physical love, taste, sound, smell, vision. All of the senses. But it helps no one to be stuck there. That's when you have worry and angst and that adds up to stress. You don't need more than enough. You just need enough.

But isn't everyone trying to figure that out—what's enough?

Well, no. Lots of people aren't stopping to think about it. They just keep greeding. Part of settin' a guideline is about listening to your own self. Which you cannot do if the body is overfed or under the influence.

This seems like a tight circle. People are supposed to listen but can't, precisely because they are overdoing. Is this especially true for white culture?

No. Everyone has their own ways of goin' too far.

What is it that you are suggesting?

I'm tellin' ya that we can't all be saved.

We can't just have heaven on earth.

No. Because then who would there be to come back and do the learnin'?

So coming back for learning is not just a karma thing?

No. It adds to the whole. Spiritual evolution.

And what is the purpose of that in the universe?

It creates more energy than there is.

It fuels something.

It's what fires the whole thing. Like in that monsters movie Monsters, Inc., *where they discovered that happy laughter had more energy value than fearful screaming. Only it's not laughter, it's about love. The capital-L Love. The big one.*

So we have to keep making that to fuel the universe. Is there danger that we won't make enough?

Tell ya, the way it's goin' now, we're headed for disaster. The whole thing is going to blow up and that'll be it.

Because the explosion will come through hatred?

Total negativity.

We need the antidote to fear.

Which is, itself, Love.

Sounds like Jesus' work.

Well, he was one of the more famous ones.

Christianity seems so spooky now.

It is bein' misused.

So is there something else?

I'm sure I thought you would never ask. Something new is on the horizon, and greedy people are going to want to get ahold of it. They think it can be worth money. There is money in it, but it's the kind of money that is shared with others, that helps everyone to get on a higher vibration. It can move a lot of people beyond survival. But money is not the key ingredient. It's about critical mass. Not of thought, but of action. It's about finding the common spirit in every one.

Common Ground.

Common ground it is. Common ground means that there is room for all.

Because we all are one.

Jimmy Cliff sings: "We all are one, we are the same person ... we all are one, same universal."

Those people, like Bob (Marley) *and Jimmy, have been singin' about it for a long time. They knew it already. If you really look inside, you have to see it. That's the part about not seeing it if you are overfed or under the influence. You have to set guidelines to get there.*

Where does Undoing Racism fit? (Undoing Racism is a curriculum that helps people understand the pervasiveness of institutional racism.)

It doesn't really, because those folks are a lot about pointing fingers. That needs to be done, too, because that's how some people will see it. But it's much bigger than that. It's about universal. It's about gathering the common threads into a quilt that covers every one. It's about understanding that we all stand on common ground. And that's the Earth. The Earth doesn't belong more to one than the other.

Lots of other cultures understand that. It's a big stretch for individualistic Westerners, who think they've earned something.

Westerners need to understand the responsibilities of stewardship.

How can this writing project help that?

To be sure, they may be interested in reading about it.

Is that beyond the scope of this channel?

Now where would you get an idea like that?

Because I feel like I'm hearing some very important ideas, but they don't seem entirely new. I don't seem to have concrete ideas to pass on.

What makes you think that everything is just going to fall in a lump in your lap? Things may take more than one visit. More than one instructor. More time to develop.

Yes, of course. I'm being impatient.

I am just a farmer, after all. I understand Common Ground intuitively. It just is.

The next conversation with **Universal Wisdom** expanded on this need to develop Common Ground. While the conversation was initially focused on my own directive to write this book, it easily applies to everyone and our collective need to focus on cultivating Life Force:

I'm assuming that this plowing is about spiritual action.

Yes. It's about movement.

Of energy?

Yes.

Starting with small focus and working toward bigger swirls.

Not just one center, but many simultaneously.

I am A Center of the Universe.

We are all centers. We need more active centers.

And centers become active by connecting.

Re-connecting to soul center, which is Love Memory. Also connecting with other centers.

Common Ground.

Common Ground. It does not make some big homogenous starburst, which is what people will want to recognize.

It's more like a nourishing stew?

No. It is We All Are One.

Recognizing one-ness in diversity.

Exactly.

And my role is?

Whatever you can. There will be different angles forming the rainbow prism.

I think of white light going through a prism and coming out a rainbow, but this is the reverse—rainbows entering the prism and coming out white light.

The white light of Love.

More Life Force. The challenge will be to bring the rainbows together into a point.

The Common Ground.

And it can happen through music, art, politics, culture shift. What about religion?

It's all possible.

So I need to choose a path.

You already have.

Writing.

It is given to you.

A gift.

It is given to you.

To be a steward.

One minute, I feel the focus. Now I am fuzzy again, wondering what to write about.

That is given, too.

Yes, *Grandmother Dreams* has been given to me. But doubt creeps in. Can I do this? Can I actually produce this book and use it to move spirit in others?

All it takes is the commitment.

Wow. I guess I need a lot of reassurance.

Whatever it takes. This is big. It's okay to go slow. It's not okay to waste time dancing around it.

It is vitally important to understand that throughout this book, the spiritual directives apply to *you*—the reader, and not just me (the typist). Always insert yourself personally into the conversations. In the conversation above, for example, Universal Wisdom is telling all of us that making the changes to evolve towards Love takes commitment.

Here, **Universal Wisdom** counsels us on the importance of faith and centering as we make the changes that shift our focus toward opening to Love:

You already have a place in the universe. Remember that. Do not be displaced from your center. That center is the root of knowing, and of knowing one another. Go deep.

I see the trees before me, rooted in the earth and swaying with the wind—they are both rooted and flexible.

And reaching—growing into the earth and toward the sun.

Thank you for guiding me so. I am moving on a path I intuit but do not see. I sense that your support is helping me move somewhere I need to be.

It is important for several reasons you are not yet aware of.

Is there anything else I should know?

You are coming into a time of great power. The kind of power that will move you in new and stronger directions. It will be important to stay centered and allow the power. Do not seek it. Let it come to you and fill you. Yes, you feel the strength. It will be many times greater. Sometimes it will be overwhelming. Stay to the center. Be the trees, and the space around them. Be the forest. Do not try to contain the power. Let it be all around you, and drink it like Life. Smile and greet it. Do not worry the details. Your job is to be it. Smile and greet it. Welcome it. Hold space for it. Don't be afraid to be big. Under your umbrella others may rest or flourish. They choose that, not you. As long as you are on center, there is enough for all.

These shifts in being have importance on a very large scale. **Universal Wisdom** outlines the coming changes and our need to not only accept them, but to be active participants in them:

There is something we want you to know about what is going to happen.

My mind is jumping quickly to questions. I am slowing down to listen—zero out my agenda.

We have talked about a change coming. This is not news. Many people know this already, many people sense it. What they don't know is what the change is. There is much discussion about the nature of the change. People assume there will be a physical calamity of some sort. That is already happening, and will continue, on the physical plane while the planet rebalances. These changes will, of course, require many adaptations. But this is not the monumental change that is on the way. Planetary rebalancing is a parallel, which is helping some to wake up to the other changes that will be necessary.

The monumental change that we are discussing is a functional change. For the purpose of simplicity, we will call it The Shift. The Shift is a rebalancing also, but it is occurring in another plane, another "dimension" if you will. Dimensions are interconnected, so changes in one will ripple into others. Because it is happening where humans cannot "see" it, there will be confusion and irritability. Humans will feel the shift but not be able to explain it in physical terms.

The Shift is necessary for cosmic balancing, there is no choosing whether you will participate or not. It will occur. It is beginning already, and will take about ten years in your time. People who are tuned in will be able to understand the changes. People who are tuned in are those who are Loving the Universe.

I am stopping to check my ego. There is the tendency to feel superior or inferior based on "tuned in enough." I know that's not what it's about.

It is, and it isn't. It is true that tuning in is required. This is a connection to what you call the spiritual world, God. It is not a religion or a religious dogma. It is not a follower-leader situation. It is about personal connection with the Love of the Universe, traveling in the Zone, movement in the Sea of Traveling Light. It is not just about heart connection, it is about Heart Open with Support of Spirit. Mind is the tool, not the medium. So, you see, it is a deeper level than most of your culture now allows. People will have to drop expectations of themselves and others in order to reach these levels. There will be a time of great learning. We hear you wondering about other cultures. Each will have its own work to do, and its own teachers. The great teachers of this time will be women. It is the time of the pendulum swinging back. It will be important to hold up that which is valuable in the feminine without trampling that which is positive in the masculine. Mistakes will be made.

It sounds a little like a return to the '60s.

The '60s were a time of excess. Principles got lost in self-serving, ego. This time will not be so much about principles as it will be about Communication. Yes, there is an explosion of communication technology now. This technology is not the kind of connection that will result in more Love. Technology is isolating, masking. People will need to learn how to talk with hearts—Honesty, Openness, Speaking Truth. These will all be necessary. Civil face-to-face dialogue will begin.

You can begin your practice right now. Every time you are with another, think: Face-to-Face, Heart-to-Heart, and Spirit-to-Spirit, My Center Meets Your Center in the Space Between Us. Reach deep, into that which you know is possible, and into that which you do not know. Accept the Mystery and let it guide you. Help yourself into the new world. Go in Peace.

"Love doesn't just sit there, like a stone.
It has to be made, like bread; remade all the time, made new."
—Ursula K. Le Guin

-2-

Creating a Home for Spirit

Universal Wisdom wants us to have a personal connection with the Love of the Universe. This connection occurs through Spirit. What is Spirit? The word *spirit* comes from the Latin *spirare*, which means "to breathe." Spirit is the vital force that characterizes a living being as being alive. When we are *in*spired, we experience both an increased mental awareness and a physical increase in energy—we are cultivating Life Force. When we *ex*pire, spirit leaves us, we die.

In order to fulfill our purpose and embody Love, our physical body must be a welcoming place for Spirit.

I once dreamed that I was visiting a Buddhist compound. When we sat for a shared meal, I realized that someone was missing—there was an empty chair. I looked out the window and saw the missing person in a field, wandering far away. He was wearing a red shirt, and I could see the red shirt growing smaller and smaller in the distance. I ran after him, calling him to come back. It was my spirit, and it had become lost. I woke up realizing that I needed to make my spirit a home, so that it would know where it belonged and it would want to be there.

What does it take for Spirit to feel welcomed, to make a home for Spirit? It is not enough to just think about making a home for Spirit—to have good intentions. We also need to prepare a physical home.

I have found it helpful to integrate an energy practice into my daily life. T'ai Chi and yoga are common forms. I use a blend of movements that focus on the spine. Twice a day, at the end of my energy practice, I invite my spirit to fill my entire being—I welcome my spirit home. My spirit appears as a cloudy energy that is vaguely the shape of my body, extending some inches beyond my visible physical boundary. I usually walk away from this practice with both me and my spirit feeling each other in movement. This is enjoyable. If you would like to learn how to work with your energy, Wendy Palmer's book *The Intuitive Body* is a good place to start.

Another place that I feel spiritually alive is out in the woods. I asked why Spirit enjoys nature so much, and the answer was that everything in nature is Spirit too—every *living* thing is Spirit expressed. Spirit enjoys that harmony. One of my Teachers had something to say about this connection to Nature:

Indian Grandfather[4]: *So this is something you are wondering about. What place you have.*
Yes, I have been thinking about identity, where I belong, sometimes not feeling comfortable anywhere but in Nature.
This is the best place to belong. Everything else comes from Nature. And there is also this human world, which appears complex. That is because it separates itself from Nature. There really is no separation. White culture's need to maintain the illusion of separation requires a lot of energy, and this creates much dysfunction. If you want to stay healthy you must stay connected with Nature, and surround yourself with others who value this. Look for ways to make yourself happy. Enjoy your relationships as much as possible. Be grateful for what you have.

---

4   There are several terms used to identify the people who were already in North America when Europeans arrived. Politically correct labels vary over time and geography. I use the term 'Indian' because the indigenous people I know use that term.

In order to welcome our spirit, we need to make choices that keep our energy clear and refreshed, to live a balanced life. In the following conversation, **Gaia**, the Supreme Goddess of the Earth, spoke about this balance:

Do I have a teacher tonight?

Yes.

Who is here?

A woman.

(A pale woman with long auburn hair and a long dress is here. She is moody, volatile, snappish, angry. She came at me with her mouth open and swallowed me head first.)

What do you have?

I have the World, and me in it.

You appear fierce.

I am nourished by beauty in Nature. Now, I am poorly fed. I am what you see when the world fails.

Storms of disasters.

Disease. Destruction.

You would like to sleep.

I am so tired. There is no rest.

What would make that possible?

Stop the pressure.

You are fighting?

I am fighting for Life Force. It is disappearing. We are out of balance. I used to have my seasons. Now I never rest. It is constant.

What would help?

Gratitude. Appreciation. Honoring. Of Life Force.

What are you?

Her immune system. Fighting off invaders and toxins. Overwhelming.

Many people lose sight of stewardship during everyday life. Things don't seem all that much different than they were just a few years ago. It's too blurry to think about what the world was like ten or twenty or two hundred years ago, either because we were younger then, with different perspectives, or we weren't alive yet.

That's why elder view is so important.

And Western culture disregards that. Focuses on youth, what's new. It's all moving so fast. It's a big job to keep up. When we focus on the fear of being left behind, we tend to lose sight of why we are trying to keep up. We lose sight of a bigger picture, the context we are functioning in, which is the Universe.

That is the allure of physical sensation, the next new thing. Status and recognition.

Ego.

Ego is running the show.

That's why kids are running many families.

And leaders are behaving like adolescents.

So if the ego is so satisfying, what would help anyone want to look beyond, to Spirit?

There has to be a connection to purpose. Spirit is about purpose, the means. The thing you do, the action you take to "make a difference." Addiction describes patterns of behavior that have more to do with the end than the means. Even if it is the act that is addictive, rather than the outcome, it is the end that satisfies the ego—it fills a need rather than a purpose. The means is about purpose.

Do I have to convince Ego that it serves Ego to make a difference?

No. You'd have to convince Spirit that Ego is necessary to make a difference. We don't want to throw out Ego, or deny it. We want to get it aligned in the best position.

To engage Spirit and align Ego, we'd have to convince people to let go of addiction?

No. You don't want to tackle addiction. You want to make it less meaningful. Decrease its reward.

By making something else appear greater.

By showing that it is possible to get high on Spirit.

Get high on Spirit?

When have you felt that?

When I see something beautiful in Nature. When I witness a very human life event, like a birth or a death. When I see a child's exuberant curiosity and innocence expressed. When I witness people connecting and loving—caring. When I connect with Universal Wisdom.

That is Love Memory.
Love Memory. If people can connect there, then that is a tool. Once people can connect there, they can help others to connect. That is how Love can spread and connect diversity. You start with those closest to connecting and ripple out from there. You don't have to do much once the ripple starts. It's just spiritual goodwill—true Love.

How do I stay spiritually open to Love and still maintain healthy boundaries? Real life is happening all of the time, and it includes both gifts and threats. What I need to survive may not be the same as what I need to live. I can't block out danger without also blocking out Life. There seems to be a relationship here with Ego. How would I be in a better place if I was functioning from Spirit?

A'Riquea : *These are all good questions to ask. Everyone struggles with this balance. We want Life to be harmonious. We go to great lengths to assure ourselves that it will be. But it is not. There is always tension between what one person wants and what another wants. It is not that one is wrong and the other is right. They are each different perspectives. True violence does occur all the time, even in nature. There are storms. There are deaths. The real point is whether we are able to accept these as part of Life. To see both the compost and the flower in all situations. To know that they are there so that we do not have to be surprised when we see them.*

This is not to say that we should not find ways to relieve injustice, or find our own path on this Earth. Part of what we are here to do is just this. The important thing is to be able to recognize what is important and what is just a distraction. What is core, and what is not. This is something that is known from the inside. It is not the same for all people, although there may be some things that affect many in the same ways, and then there will be a mass change.

It is important to listen to what our Spirit is telling us. Spirit knows what is core and what is not. Spirit also knows the healing ways when there is pain. You must ask your Spirit to be your guide. It will be willing when it is invited. Being open means being open to Spirit —your own and that of others. The role of Ego is to enjoy that which Spirit chooses.

When Ego does the choosing, that un-invites Spirit. Ego chooses for its own enjoyment. That is pleasure for pleasure's sake. It begins to cloud Inner Wisdom. When Spirit chooses, it is for All. When Ego allows Spirit to choose, Ego's enjoyment will support movement on the Soul's path. Alignment fosters harmony. The very harmony we seek is available in every moment.

True religious practice is spiritual practice. It welcomes Spirit, it opens to Spirit, and Ego enjoys Spirit. Mass religion cannot provide this. It is only individual practice that invites Spirit, whether that is in the context of religion or not. Christianity attempts to place Spirit outside, as if it is something that is gifted to us only under special circumstances. Spirit is a gift, but that is the nature of Life. It is present in every person. Everyone's spirit is connected to many dimensions, but it is primarily personal in the physical realm. One can invite personal spirit by making a home for it-—in one's own body. That is why it is said that the body is a temple. Once personal spirit is well established, larger connections may be made. Personal spirit comes first.

Balance is an important part of establishing personal spirit. Many of the conversations referred to this balance by using a train analogy. The train analogy describes a balance among three parts—Ego, Spirit, and Soul—which are all necessary for spiritual evolution. The Ego is the engine, the physical body that makes movement of any kind of energy possible in this physical dimension. Spirit is the fuel, the motivation, behind any action taken on the spiritual path. The optimum fuel is Love. Soul is the track, the path itself, the movement of healing and the expression of God through Life Force.

Many self-help gurus would like us to believe that the Ego is the problem, that Ego is in the way of spiritual development, and that if we just got rid of its interference then all would be well. The Ego itself is not the problem. How the Ego functions determines whether or not we will cultivate Life Force. Ego in service to itself, feeding the "me first" part of our personality that craves approval and control, will ultimately be destructive. Addiction describes this imbalance—the engine will run poorly and does not travel the path of the Soul. When Ego is in service to Spirit, the motivation supporting choice of action is Love, a connection with the All. This is the fuel that supports compassionate action, and nourishes Life Force. This is our true spiritual purpose.

Here, **Universal Wisdom** uses the train analogy to discusses addiction:
Are the terms addiction and Ego interchangeable?
No. Addiction is Ego in incorrect position. Ego itself is an important component. But it needs context to operate properly.
The context is Spirit?
Spirit is balancing. Either engine or fuel alone does not run the train. Both are needed.
So addiction is not a good fuel blend.
It runs too hot. The engine overheats. The body is limited in a way it doesn't need and cannot tolerate.
The Ego needs to be motivated to action by appropriate spiritual energy.
Ego is action. The fuel/motivation determines the choice of actions. Self-serving or spirit-serving.
Which is why a twelve-step program can work—because it pulls the focus into a bigger view, something larger than self.
Yes. Although too often the twelve-step programs becomes the next addiction. One needs to recognize addiction as a process, a cycle. Not the circle of Life.

This discussion about creating balance between the Ego and the Spirit with the use of the train analogy continued in another conversation with **Universal Wisdom**:

I have been working with over-soul communication, the opportunity to communicate with other spirits without the limits of our physical realm. This is a way to further expand my mind.
Not your mind. Your Soul.
Hmmm. In the train analogy, Soul was the track, the path.

31

It's an energy path that can pick up and drop off passengers.
Sharing experience.
Sharing Love.
Resonance.
Resonance is the fuel, Spirit.
So is path predestined?
Path is the movement, Life Force.
I'm thinking of plant growth, how there is a perseverance in reaching toward growth that seems to be hardwired, and then there are all of the events that affect the growth during the plant's life—drought, storms, animal grazing, winter, crowding—and give it its unique shape.
This is true of humans, too.
The nature-nurture dance. But Life Force, the originator—this is Soul?
Yes.
And we have talked before about Life Force and Love.
Love is the evidence of Life Force. Love is how Life Force manifests.
We are programmed for it. But Life Force and Love are not the same?
They are the same, and they are different.
Can you explain?
Not yet.
So over-soul communication has something to do with reuniting Soul/Life Force. What is an over-soul?
The path that the soul would have taken without the effects of life on it.
Connecting to the original.
I need to clarify:

> Ego is the engine, the action, the physical manifestation.
> Spirit is the fuel, the resonance, the motivation, Love.
> Soul is the energy path, the movement, Life Force.

Am I getting this?
Yes.
But is physical manifestation also Spirit and Soul?
It can be. Holiness requires presence. Presence is acceptance of Spirit, which allows the movement of Soul.
And it's not all in there to begin with?

Of course. When one awakens to Spirit, it allows Soul to move. Putting the Ego in charge puts the Spirit to sleep, and limits Soul movement.

What is it about Life Force movement that is important to the Universe?

It is a renewable energy source, which can be put into new projects.

But I wonder if that is like the government and gross national product, as if we always need to keep producing and making more. That is a limited outlook.

It depends what you are producing.

Life force fuels other dimensions.

Indirectly, yes.

I have always been curious about this planet Earth—what if it was actually just a cell or a molecule in the scheme of things, and all of the activity here was important for the function of something else, something so big we can't even conceive of it because we are so small.

That's the idea.

Look at the photos of deep space. We are teensy in perspective. There is all of this arrogant importance placed on the existence of humans here. Are we really that big a deal?

Yes, but for a different reason. Not because humans are so much better than any other life form on Earth, but because humans fill a specific niche in something bigger.

What are we?

The powerhouses of Love.

So the Earth is a cell in something much larger, and it is populated by beings that are also made up of cells. When I asked about cellular memory, I was given the words "many spirits." Apparently, Life Force/Spirit essence is retained in cells.

Universal Wisdom: *No. Each cell has a spirit, too. Your spirit is made up of all of these together.*

So illness has something to do with a disorganized whole?

Which may be due to something more than the whole or the parts are able to handle.

33

I have also been thinking of trauma and dissociation. Does the Spirit actually leave the body?

No. Because then the body would die. But parts of the Spirit do leave, parts of consciousness.

So the mind is Spirit too.

The brain is the body. The mind is where Spirit connects to the body.

Not in the cells.

There too. But the body cannot be aware of Spirit without the mind.

And awareness is important because that is how Spirit is fed—by knowing what feeds Spirit and choosing that.

Yes.

I feel that many circumstances have collaborated in the last few years of my life to increase my awareness, and I have been able to make spirit-feeding choices. I feel healthier than I ever have.

That is the absence of toxins, movement toward better sleep and nutrition, and exercise. Plus choice.

Yes. I do feel like the more I choose this, the more I want to choose it.

It helps itself. Choosing toxins goes the other direction. Substance use limits spiritual connection. With limited connection, people feel lost. They choose more toxin to cover up the feelings of loss.

I am working with a quit-smoking group right now.

Smoking is toxic on a chronic basis, like being an alcoholic, only nicotine is the drug. All of the behaviors with it just support the toxin choice. A life is built around the toxin, instead of around the spirit.

Most people would find that difficult to see.

Until they un-choose the toxin.

Bring that back to the discussion of every cell having a Spirit.

Yes. The toxin—in this case, nicotine—disrupts each cell's spirit, as well as the communication, the harmony, between cells. Remember that Spirits enjoy harmony. Their interactions feed each other. When each cell-spirit is disrupted and communication is disharmonized, that is when cancer develops. Like losing their place in the music.

Is cancer always environmental?

It is always chemical, and chemical is energy too. Toxin can result from stress and trauma. Stress and trauma can be mitigated by attitude— belief, perspective.

Are awareness and consciousness the same thing?

Awareness is more surface, does not go as deep as consciousness. Consciousness is also cellular.

Are there things smaller than cells that are also Spirit? I always wonder if molecules or atoms are like solar systems, with their own planets and living beings and more cells and so on.

The earth is a cell.

This can go endlessly in both directions—macro and micro.

The quantity is not as important as the quality. Right now quality is declining, disorganizing, because the natural world is being disregarded and it cannot communicate as it needs to—with itself. Gaia principles are sound.

(Current Gaia theory views earth as a single organism, with all the components of earth and its biosphere interacting to create a self-regulating homeostasis—balance.)

Is it too late for our planet?

It is never too late. The less is addressed, the more destruction will occur in the imbalance. There will be no Armageddon, just greater and greater disruption in the current arrangement. Your own sobriety is a good example. It takes time to un-choose toxins and heal the whole. At some point, that feels good and becomes self-perpetuating. This can happen on many levels: personal, community, habitat, cultures, ecosystems, planet.

Addiction, choosing toxins, does not just describe imbalanced relationships with objects or substances. It can also include feelings and reactions. Here is an example, as discussed with **Universal Wisdom:**

My tao reading today said, "Worry is an addiction that inhibits compassion." Worry feeds the cycle of being afraid, that there won't be enough, that there will be too much, that I won't be able to handle it, that I won't be in control. It presupposes a negative environment and then creates one, by constantly imagining scenarios of negativity that require chronic vigilance. Is the opposite of worry safety?

No. Balance.
Ego in the right position.
Yes.
It would be foolish to be naive to danger. Equally foolish to immerse myself in it. The middle ground is—*Balance.*
Yet balance seems like such a vague term. I can visualize a fulcrum or a scale with opposite ends balanced.
Think Nonduality.
It's not one or the other, not black or white.
It's an "and" proposition.
Addiction attempts to allay fear, by creating the illusion of comfort, but actually creates more fear with the danger-worry cycle of losing that comfort.
List areas in your own life.
Worry, of course. Junk food, sugar—the illusion of contentment; but the more I use the further I distance myself from physical balance, and thus from actual contentment. In my youth, I used drugs and alcohol to escape, and smoked pot in the hopes of making a spiritual connection. But toxin buildup eventually inhibits clarity of mind. A lot of it is about toxin buildup. With emotions, too. This occurs anytime one area is used to the detriment of others.
Imbalance.
I'd have to include sex, too.
Once again, balance. Sex is a good part of being in the physical plane. It is made to enjoy, but using it without balance in other life areas, such as emotional intimacy, creates imbalance.
Which describes addiction.
Addiction describes an imbalance.
There are other ways to be out of balance.
Like poor health.
How does that work?
It is a challenge beyond balance, into other energy frames.
Culture is better able to support some than others—physical illness more so than mental illness, for example.
They are the same.
In energy work?

No. In balance work. All of it is important. Don't get distracted by culture. That is beyond the individual.

It's important to work where Life is.

Where Love is.

The purpose of balance is to strengthen Love, Life Force.

Yes.

I'm thinking about common "news" stories that are really just hyper-sexualized media. It's up to each one of us to say, "No, I'm not buying this. I'm turning this off. I'm investing in something else."

Yes.

It is alluring because it is titillating.

There's the addiction.

It seems to me that most of the hyper-sexualized media market is fueled by the male-animal-hormone-response thing.

Men have different balancing issues than women. Women are part of this market too because women choose to be the objects and also to compare themselves to objects and buy into the addiction of feeding the male response.

Everyone is involved.

Yes. The outcome is that now children are involved too. Children are sexual creatures, but it is on a different level than adults. Child sexuality is being directed into adult behavior.

It's TV—that other addiction.

They all feed each other.

They are connected.

Negatively.

This feels like a huge area to tackle.

Unless you bring it down to individuals—addiction, balance, Life.

We would all like to think that we are making good choices. It is hard to look inside and see the ways that we are creating our own imbalances. The following story gives us a humorous glimpse into an extreme situation of denial:

Is there anyone who wants to talk today? There is a big crowd, all with their hands waving excitedly. Okay, **Angela**, you seem the most exuberant. She got mad because I wrote "pushy" first and then changed it to exuberant. I'm sorry, honey. If you want to talk, you can, but I'm not going to chase you around today. Of course I'm interested in what you've got. It's all good.

Well, I was gonna tell you about this time I was at my mother's house. We were all getting ready for a big meal. Like at a holiday. People was tryin' to be loving, but there was a lot of fussin', too. Wouldn't you know that little cousin of mine was foolin' around and brought his knife point down and stabbed it right through my brother's hand who had it sittin' on the table. The whole room went silent in shock. Like a big gasp. The cousin couldn't believe what he'd done. He looks around at everyone lookin' at him and says, "I didn't do it!" He still got the knife in his fist and everything. The whole place just busted out laughing. How dumb can you get? He still got a big ol' whuppin' anyway.

Denial helps us to move our focus away from thoughts and behavior that make us uncomfortable. It can take many forms. In the following exchange, **Universal Wisdom** helped me see how my own behavior was not only limiting resolution, but also describing an addiction— my choice to stay angry was creating an imbalance:

I ended a twenty-year relationship with a person who used avoidance and intentional deceit as coping skills. Years later, he still behaves this way. Even though I can't expect that pattern to change, I still react with anger. When I have to communicate with him I feel a need to state my concerns, but it is difficult to keep it factual and unemotional. Why bring up my concerns at all?

He does need to see the ripple effects of his choices.

Why am I still so angry? So hurt?

Anger is a choice. Hurt is a need.

Anger is choice, a choice of reaction. I could be depressed or victimized or enraged. I choose anger. Hurt is a need—a need to feel respected?

A need to feel honored as a living human being with feelings. That did not happen in this relationship.

I feel like he never actually loved me. He only used me to get whatever he needed.

That is true.

And it is still true now.

No.

What is different?

He is afraid of you. Afraid of you taking his children, of you being more connected in the community. He is weak and he knows it.

That is an interesting angle. It does feel like a lot of what I want to say to him is accusing, and maybe I just want to point out what I see.

That would be better.

And what is it that I see? I see that he is not supporting our children emotionally, that he is not sharing responsibility for making sure that there is food in their house, that he is using the woman he had an affair with to be the parent he doesn't know how to be.

He is using her as a crutch.

To not have to develop himself, to not have to look at some difficult things in his own life. He does not want to admit the significance of the damage done to our family.

He knows it. He wants to look away. You are a reminder.

Just like he is a reminder for me.

There is a lot of pain here.

Maybe it would be good to acknowledge that.

It would be better to state your feelings. Not just your feelings, but how you see the situation.

When I think that way I feel empowered. Not controlling, but more in myself, more who I am, more centered. I give myself permission to have those feelings instead of thinking that I have to move beyond them. I acknowledge them, and then I can move along into something healthier, something that includes them but is not limited to them, stepping into a bigger picture.

Jennifer Shoals

Acknowledge your losses, then re-center and place them in the context of your Life.

> "Letting go is not a technique. Letting go is an
> outcome that follows a shift in attention."
> —Wendy Palmer

Letting go requires that we look at something and see it in context. Sometimes the things that are holding us back are unseen. I participated in a ritual that moved me deeply and exposed a wound I had not been aware of. In looking at this wound, **Universal Wisdom** helped me to see how Ego can be out of balance not just by over-feeding, but also by under-feeding self—by denying self:

A mirror was propped so that I could see myself and my women friends standing behind me at the same time. In the exercise, I listened to them sing to me as I looked at myself in the mirror. They sang these words:

How could anyone ever tell you that you're anything less than beautiful?

How could anyone ever tell you that you're less than whole?

How could anyone fail to notice the loveliness of your spirit?

How deeply you have touched me in my soul.

I was unable to look at myself in the mirror. I cried through most of the song. I was forced to see a broken place in myself—I could not believe that I was beautiful. What about the pain of looking in the mirror? What is that then? Is that Ego/personality, or Spirit?

That is Spirit showing you itself, and you being unwilling to look.

It is so easy to see the beauty of spirit in others. There was not one woman there that I could not see when it was her turn in the mirror. Why is it so hard to look at my own self?

Because you have no practice.

I need more affirmations?

It's not just a mantra. It's a way of being, that includes you in the family of humans. You think that you are outside of that family, that you don't belong. It doesn't really matter where that comes from. There are many pieces contributing to that. The important thing is to take your place.

Where do I belong now? I know that I belong in the world of Spirits. I am trying to fit in human form, and this is difficult.

All humans struggle with this. Balancing how much Ego and how much Spirit. This is what we have been talking about.

How can it be that I have not enough Ego?

That isn't the issue. The issue is what you do with that Ego. How do you use it. To push yourself down. That is another misuse of Ego.

I usually think of ego out of place as overeating, but this is about starving, which is clearly how I under-function in many areas of my life— under-eating, under-sleeping, over-giving—denying myself.

You need to feed yourself.

That is scary—feeding myself, taking up space. It feels selfish.

Yet there is unlimited space.

I don't see that. I'm at plenty of gatherings where there is the know-it-all space hog. No one else can talk or interact.

And that is too much. What about taking the form that you occupy and making it more spacious. Having more space. Embodying Love means that you fill yourself, not with stuff, but with space. It is hard to maintain that much space without a foundation of physical grounding.

I do understand that. I'm wondering how rest builds physical grounding.

By giving the body a break from physical control. Being involuntary. Like a muscle, it is easier to understand relaxation in the context of contraction, and vice versa. Yin and yang. Going just one direction is not useful. You need to know that stress is cumulative. And so is rest.

In another conversation, **Universal Wisdom** outlined why it is so important to take our place in the family of humans and also in the spirit world:

We've talked a fair amount about Ego and Spirit, the purpose of Love. Is there a missing piece?

Not a missing piece, but a fuller picture.

Yes, that would be good. Some kind of bigger context?

It is already in context. What you need to start thinking about is how this applies to the present. People will need a thread that weaves it all together.

Is that something you can help me with?

Yes. We can do this today.

I am listening.

This is the way the world works: You come in on a kind of contract, an agreement. You agree to do your best to keep shining under the circumstances. This contract is forgotten once you enter the physical world, because there are so many distractions. But everyone's job involves keeping the contract. Manifesting God's Pure Love on earth produces a kind of energy that cannot be produced elsewhere in the Universe. There are other energies being produced, but not at this vibration. People on earth feel lost and depressed when they are out of touch with this vibration. They feel exalted when they are connected. Connection is difficult to maintain. It requires regular practice and attention.

It is true that Life is where you put your attention. The Middle East is a miasma because so many are focused on reaction and anger. The United States is encouraging that. American culture is also encouraging numbness of its own population, so that there are consumer sheep. The work involves waking people up to their true nature, not the shutdown or blown-out reaction. Nobody wants to be told what to do. There is an automatic defense when told that your way is wrong. There needs to be some way to build on what is already there, even if it is in little pieces.

The wake up will lift the veil. There are already many people working on this. It is having some effect. That's why adding to it is important. You have been told before that you have a place in this. So does everyone else. Do not take your responsibility too heavily. Your job is to provide the information. Ultimately, it is up to them to choose to change. What you must do is create a kind of mirror, which they are not afraid to look into. You will be in there with them.

I am thinking of the beauty ritual, with my sisters' faces surrounding me, and I was unable to look in.

Use that example. Show how it is difficult to look. Because it is so intense. There needs to be ways to reduce the fear.

So where are these tools going to come from?

From yourself. You will need to do the work of looking in the mirror, and finding out what needs to happen for that to go forward. Once that is complete, you will be ready to organize the book.

Of course, that sounds like a scary task. I do see the connection, though. If I am going to ask others to do this, then I need to be able to do it myself and to provide some tools or guidelines for that. Seeing our beauty, for example.

Seeing inside.

Hmm. Which is what happens with this meditative writing, connection to Universal Wisdom, the *Grandmother Dreams*.

Exactly.

I have been wondering about that—if it really is within reach of the average person. It seems a little far out.

It is far out. That is why people need to reconnect to it. Not everyone will accept this. Remember that you are writing for those who are already on this path. This is a support. Preach to the choir, but show them some new songs.

This sounds like a link to Star Sky Forever.

This will be included.

That is part of the looking in?

Yes, but it is not the whole picture. If that was enough, you would not be instructed to learn how to look in the mirror.

It could be a foundation but not the full action.

Yes.

Would it be good to get outside input on this?

Maybe, but you are dancing around the directive. Y-O-U need to look in the mirror.

Yes, yes. I'm putting up blocks.

Use the hand mirror.

I will. Thank you.

I was asked to think about the mirror, and that helped me become aware of the many times I was judging others. Being in close contact with my extended family over the holidays was a perfect opportunity to see that. Each time I would hear myself making a judgment (which implies placing a negative label), I held up the mirror to my own self and asked, "Am I perfect? What traits do I exhibit that drive someone else crazy? What is there about myself that I can't or don't see? Who am I to judge?" I just remembered the discussion some time ago about the word "judge," as in "to place a value on." That "judge not" means to "make room for." I also remember the information about Star Sky Forever, and how I used to look at others and ask myself if they were a star in my Universe. Because the field of the Universe is unlimited, every single person is a star in my sky. I am a star too. So far, that is what I have figured out on my own about the mirror. I wonder what else needs to be known.
I will listen now.

Universal Wisdom: *Good. You have done well. There are a lot of pieces there that you can put to good use in this chapter. The mirror is about judgment. You see well when you are looking out at others. You do not see well when you are looking at yourself. You are still uncomfortable looking in, because you are not able to control the tendency to judge self.*
Yes. I feel jittery when I look. I cannot take the gaze for long, and I jump away.
Yet you are sitting now and listening. Where do you think this comes from?
That is a good question. I have often wondered. Is it me? Is it inside coming out or outside coming in, or both?
It is both, but there is also a part that is just inside. I hear you feeling uncomfortable with taking credit for anything.
I was taught that pride is a "sin."
Being boastful and full of yourself at the expense of others is not helpful. That is Ego out of place. Remember that we have been talking about Ego in the most helpful position. That means that you need to be grounded in the physical world. Healthy is another word for grounded. Good health implies balance.

Yes, I remember talking about using my turn in this life well—paying attention to rest, sleep, diet, exercise. I feel it now—fear when the focus is turned on to me, not as a spirit presence on a soul path but as a physical manifestation of me. What is it about me that I find so intimidating? *Responsibility.*

I am responsible for my actions and choices. That is not hard for me—that is what integrity is. I have a deep respect for that. In myself and others.

There is another kind of responsibility.

I must know what it is, because my fear is mounting. I want to keep talking to keep it from coming. I need to be still and open.

There is a billboard with a picture of Gandhi on it that reads, "Justice is not just something you talk about. It is something you work for."

This is the responsibility you need to be more aware of. The responsibility to take action. Not just to do good works, but to do them with awareness and purpose. You are already experienced with good works. You understand the benefits to yourself and others. It is time to put this ability into a bigger context, to see a bigger picture and put it into motion through practice. You cannot just be a do-gooder. You have to be an agent for positive change. All of it requires that the Ego be placed in balance. Remember that the Ego is the engine. Spirit is the fuel. The engine goes nowhere without fuel. And the Spirit needs a vehicle to take action.

This is becoming clearer. Ego is the engine, the action. Spirit is the fuel, but the fuel for what?

Love.

Here we are again. When action is fueled by Love, the soul path is being traveled.

Yes. And Soul path being traveled produces more Love. It is not only fueled by Love but also produces it. It is an important cycle.

It is what you have been telling me about—the need to embody Love.

Yes. It is not that you are going to save something, although that will happen too. It is that you need to develop this path.

I see this in the context of the book. It's not just about helping people decide to balance Ego, to become spiritually aware. It's about cultivating more agents for positive change—to convince others of the path of Love, which is not just talking the talk but doing something about it.

45

Exactly.

Why would this process seem so frightening to me and, I assume, to others?

It requires you to expand your energy body and then put your ego to work through it. You, and others, instinctually know the dangers of expanding. Increased visibility can make you more vulnerable, place you at risk. It leads to persecution by those whose disproportionately large piece of the pie is threatened when others become aware. Women and people of color know this in their bones. The stories of what happens when you stand up are still in their cells. But stand up you must for good to grow. You must use examples like Gandhi, who stood up despite the danger, because it was the right thing to do.

Take note of how much Ego it requires to manage that bigger life. Not Ego in the negative sense, of greed and gluttony, but the positive Ego, which allows you to move through life. Balanced Ego. Ego that knows its service is to Spirit. You must practice expanding your energy. Make sure not to dilute it. Expand only as far as you can and still maintain spatial density. Practice living this way. You will need to feed your physical body as well as your Spirit to maintain this. Plan for maintenance in order to develop new habits.

Thank you. It is so helpful to get this in stages. I feel ready to do this.

Go slow.

One of the first places to look at judgment, then, is my own view of myself. It is easy to see faults in others, and much more difficult to be objective about my inner world. The following exchange helped me look there and heal my shame:

Some days I feel a little crazy. I am so far into the dream world that I am somewhat detached from the physical world. I do not doubt what is happening for a minute. And I see how the information applies to the physical world. But integrating the experiences is still new. So here I am.

Indian Grandfather has his arms folded, and he is nodding toward **Healing Grandmother.** She is facing me, motioning for me to come to her with both her arms. So I am walking to her. She is holding her arms out, open, to me. She hugs me gently and strokes my hair. She is pointing behind me, up toward the sky. Then she points back at me. She is explaining something. I cannot hear her words, only see her mouth move. She turns me round, and I see her pointing to the sky over my left shoulder. It is a daytime sky with clouds. *This is the way you must go*, she says. *If you want to see your Eagle Brother, you must go this way. Don't be afraid to leave your body.*

I see myself floating up, and I am the spirit woman I know as Flower Stream—the feminine embodiment of my essence. Healing Grandmother has her hand on my shoulder, indicating that she will keep my body behind. I am up in the air, and I look back to see Healing Grandmother's hand on the shoulder of Flower Stream. So now I am just the spirit me. I feel light … and free. My mind is beginning to cloud and lose focus. I could get lost up here. Grandmother is shouting some instructions: *Don't be afraid. Go without fear.* I feel my warrior spirit zooming. *Don't push*, she yells. Maybe I should go back and learn before leaving? *Follow the Life Force*, she tells me. I can hear her in my ear.

I can see the earth below. The trees are sending off green sparks. There are red trails coming up from humans—that is Love. I see yellow swirling amongst them, healing energy. I feel my own Life Force, a thin red thread trailing behind me. Thread is spinning out as I swim forward. A purple thread is spinning out ahead of me like a tendril seeking ground. It is a flat purple ribbon, and I am following it. I can hear a Paul LaRouche song. I am transforming from Flower Stream, the buckskin dress long around my heels, my hair untied and streaming. The purple ribbon is curling into the clouds far ahead of me. Rainbows are streaming off of my head instead of my hair. My hands are reaching forward, glowing green. Songs are coming from my mouth, words I do not yet know. I am smiling and reeling in the purple ribbon with my hand like I am plucking a harp. I see my purple ribbon pulling, a man at the end of it, the ribbon curled gently around his waist.

It is **Eagle Brother**, and he is smiling. He has his hands parked behind his head, as if he is enjoying the ride. And then he is very close. As if our energy paths have crossed over each other. He is behind me now. I feel soft and ethereal. He is pulling the ribbon, which is still tied around his waist, to pull me closer. I am floating and laughing. There is some aggression in his pull, some anger in his face. I am next to him now and give him a soft kiss on his right cheek. He is angry, as if he did not want to be pulled in. I change my image back to the me he can recognize, the me who was on the bleachers at pow-wow. He looks startled, and then perplexed. I am Woman, I say. Are you the Man I see?

No, he replies, *I am all the Men you see.* He raises his palms up and looks to the sky.

We are the Sun, and the burning power of the Sun. We bring Light to the Earth.

He motions all around him in the golden yellow sunlight.

We are the bringers of Light. You, he continues, *are all of the Women. You are the Earth, the soil and the land, Home. When we join, there is great power, for that is when Life is made. The two powers work together. When the two powers do not work together, then there is darkness and chaos. Harmony is important, True Harmony. It cannot be pretended. We are in a time now where there is Harmony around the edges, but not in the center. Men will have to give up some power in order to share, in order to create balance. We are afraid of this. It is why I am sometimes angry with you. Because I see the face of the future on your face. It tells me that I must find a new way to be a warrior. The current way does not bring Harmony. This new way is a shift in feelings. Men do not have the tools for this. Women can share tools. That is less threatening than just taking control. Taking control leads to imbalance. You must find a way to share tools. The tools we need are Talking Hearts.* He looks deflated, face downcast. *That is why I looked to you at pow-wow, I thought we could Talk Hearts.*

I wanted to Talk Hearts, too, I say. We did not get that far. I saw your heart, and it was beautiful, and then I had to leave and could not come back. I still want to Talk Hearts. I have been sad that I did not know where to find you. I am glad you are here. Can we Talk

Hearts now? (He peers at me curiously.) I am curious. What happens to your heart when you are dancing in the circle?

(He is radiant, and his arms spread wide open.)

My heart grows big, outside my physical body. The sun and the earth join in my body, and I am happy to be alive. I wondered why you did not dance.

Now it is my turn to look down. I feel ashamed. I have white skin. I enjoy dancing, for then I become a spoke in the Wheel of Life. I am not sure of being welcome in the native circle, and I do not want to offend anyone by taking a place that does not belong to me. I desperately want to dance, to feel that oneness and completion. He takes my chin in his thumb and forefinger and lifts my face so that I can look into his eyes. I am afraid to look.

Look at me.

Tears are coming. I am not worthy. My face is up, but my eyes cannot meet his. I am ashamed to be White.

Look at me.

I cannot. I cannot face my shame. Forgive me, please, I whisper. He lets his hand drop and turns to walk away. Can I let him leave just to protect my own shame?

I will look, I say to his back. He comes before me again, holds one of my hands in each of his. He wears the cloth headband like Grandfather. I am wiping my tears. I take a deep breath, breathe slowly into the earth.

I am filled, with Love, I say out loud. I can now look into his eyes. They are strong. There are lightning flashes around the edges. The pupils are white, with white eagles circling in them. Now they are red, the color of the sacred pipe. They are yellow, like the sunrise. They are blue, like the September sky. They are black, like the night sky, and they are full of stars.

Am I a star in your sky?

Yes.

Are you a star in your sky? (He asks a little forcefully.)

I am hesitant to say yes. What is this?

I am a star in my sky, I state assertively.

You see then, there are all colors, and they are all stars. When you honor the Circle, you are welcome in it. Please come.

He holds his right hand out to me. I take his hand. It is warm and smooth. I work to keep my eyes from falling down again. I am following him through the clouds. We are walking. He stops and pulls me in front of him, both facing forward. He leans over, his head at my right ear, his left hand pointing over my left shoulder into the sky.

That is the way.

His quiet voice reassures me. I look up where his finger is pointing. The clouds have parted and blue sky is visible behind. He comes around to face me and tenderly kisses me on the mouth. I am touched by this. I gently kiss him back, sending Love. We are quietly in each other's arms. He caresses my forehead with his lips. I lean my head down to his chest. I can hear his Heart Talking. He smiles.

We land softly with our feet on the ground. We squeeze each other's hands and turn our opposite directions. I see Grandmother with her hand on Flower Stream's shoulder. I dive back into my body and Grandmother gives me a playful shove away from her. She is laughing.

And here I am in my living room.

One aspect of shame is the need to self-punish—based on the belief that because I am a bad person, it is reasonable that bad things happen to me. I came to a point, however, where I began to wonder just how much suffering was enough. This conversation with **Universal Wisdom** was helpful:

Am I somehow wired to believe that I should suffer?
It became wired.
The experience created the circuit, which has been reinforced over and over by my behavior.
It is a major pathway now.
Which is part of this learning—uncovering the belief that I don't deserve to be loved. I am afraid to allow love because I really don't

deserve it? No—afraid because I don't know how to trust it. The trust path is unused, small and low-current. I feel uneasy using it. It would be good to practice using it. Fear is a resistor. How is electrical resistance overcome? Remove the resistor or increase the current. I'm pretty sure that a blowout from too much current is too drastic, not a healing move. I need to decrease power to the suffering pathway. I want to gradually increase current on the trust pathway. What does it take to trust? Some level of safety. Some understanding that life happens and it's not all so personal. Some courage to move toward Love. Whoa. That feels scary. So I will try saying it again. Trusting requires the courage to move toward Love. I have often heard that courage is not the absence of fear—it is the knowledge that something else is more important. What is more important that I need to see? *Love is the Life Force. Flow of Life Force improves health and creativity, and increases your ability to share Love with others.*

This is something I can easily agree with from a functional point of view. Just this week, I was saying that I need to make a living but my primary work goal is to be in a position to make a difference. This is where Love and Life Force come in, because the most important thing in helping others help themselves is to be as Loving as possible. I can see the personal limits that I have come up against—having good intentions but being uneasy with follow-through, uneasy with making the personal and lasting connections that make a difference. Because I have feared that I am not good enough, I have not trusted myself, I have held back when I get to a certain point in relationships. My current job is a good place to practice courage.

I can still feel the fear, so I know I have come to a growing edge here. It is even more glaring when I move off of the secondary point of professional spiritual development and try to look at the more primary point of my personal life. My core, my inner self, is very defensive about opening to Love. I certainly have loving, intimate relationships with my children. Right now, that has a level of safety defined by their developmental ages. Maybe later in life I would share more of myself, but it is not appropriate with younger people who need me to support them, not have them support me. When I extend myself farther, into a peer relationship—like with a lover, that scares me. I am seeing for the first time how I hide behind sex, because sex feels like intimacy. But how often have I and my partner shared a deep emotional intimacy before becoming sexual? I chalk that up to males, who are "not really capable of going there." That's partly true and partly a self-fulfilling judgment—I choose partners who can't connect, or I don't let them into my inner life, and then it never works out. Imagine that.

I assume that if these areas of spiritual intimacy could be opened, the rest would all just fall in place. But am I ready or able to be courageous? I feel that I need to acknowledge the fear and still move ahead. Slowly, of course. I need to Love myself in the growing process.

In acknowledging the fear, I have seen the edge of it. I am afraid that if I open to Love, I will be hurt. That is the reinforced history. There are many layers. I don't have to see myself as damaged. I need to see myself as hurt, wounded, possibly disabled in some ways. All the more reason to be patient and gentle. But I cannot give up, cannot discard my healing as impossible.

It is okay to say yes to someone's love. You do not need to feel embarrassed if they are not exactly what you had in mind. They are what you need right now. They are a gift from the Universe. Be grateful. See how it goes.

Balance is not just about facing my shame or rebuilding my ability to trust. Balance requires that I practice self-care, that I feed myself Love.

Healing Grandmother has been waiting for me. She is at the window of unknowing. She is pointing into it with a little smile on her face. It makes me smile too. So here I go. She gives me a playful push as I go through. I'm in the mist. I'm enjoying the expansion of my energy, the spaciousness of not being limited by physical form. My face is upturned and my eyes are closed. I am streaming upward, my hair blowing straight behind me, my arms down at my sides and slightly out, with my palms down and fingers outward. I am wearing white. My feet are bare. This feels very angelic.

Universal Wisdom: *You are an angel.*

My eyes pop open with fear—that would be a big responsibility!
Look how you react.
I'm worried that somehow I'm not strong enough, I won't be able to do it. Yet this angel-ness is how I feel when I am with others. What is an angel?
An angel is a helper, a guide—selfless and compassionate. An angel moves to where there is need. An angel gives and Loves.
I think of an angel as a spirit form. I am a human.
A human angel. You have chosen this role.
Is it okay to be playing a role?
Not if you are playing. Only if you are sincere.
I feel sincere. But I am so tired. This cannot be good for my body, all this giving.
You have removed many barriers this week. It is important to rest.
Are there also some guidelines to remember?
There are. You must be available to yourself in the same way that you make yourself available to others.
Compassionate.
Loving. You cannot give others what you are not willing to give to yourself.
There is a saying: " Do not wish for me what you do not wish for yourself."
It is not wishing. It is giving.
I avoid Love. It makes me feel uncomfortable when it is directed at me.
Love feeds your Spirit. You cannot go without it. It is like a plant without sunshine. You must seek it. Drink it in. Big-L Love.
May I be filled with Love, that I may spread Love. I would like to use this as a mantra. Choose a number of times to repeat it out loud. What else?
Ask for Love.
Sounds vague. Oh, but I immediately thought of it as a direct question to another person.
That would be one way.
But I could also send it out into the Universe, the space where I oversoul.
Yes.

"Could I please have some Love?" That sounds like begging. How about "I am ready for Love"?

Love is an energy.

Then I would ask for a transfer, a deposit into my account. But I usually am so tight on cash. I want an account that overflows, that has no limits. I want to win the Love lottery. I want—that sounds so egotistical. What would the Spirit say?

The spirit would say it is time for more Love. Think about the sunshine parallel.

Yes. I make efforts to get outside, to make sure my skin is exposed, to make sure I get enough time in the sun. In other words, I go where the sun is and make sure I am in it. If I was going to go where the Love is, that would be … nature. But I need human input. Where is Love? Unconditional Love?

Love is where the heart is open.

Meditation.

That's one place.

Massage.

Good start.

I'm getting the point that it's about receiving—practicing receiving. It includes being present physically.

Of course.

I do hug a lot.

This is good.

Many short answers—I'm not exactly hitting the mark here.

No.

Oh. Touched by God.

Yes.

I need to practice connecting there. So I just did that. Was it a self-created sensation?

Only you know that.

The mantra that goes with this is "*I am filling with Love.*"

This conversation about self-care continued on another day:

If receiving from others feels so good, then why would I avoid it?

Universal Wisdom: *Because you have to be vulnerable to go there.*

Going to that very deep place.

That is why you need to practice. It needs to be easy to go there. That is how you will get what you need.

And that would be more satisfying to my partner as well, if I was able to accept what they had given to me.

Yes, but the reason to do it is to refuel yourself.

Immediately, I feel selfish about that.

But you have to refuel. Avoiding it makes you ill.

Balance.

Exactly.

This refueling is what we have been talking about for months, feeding Spirit.

Yes. And it is not some concept outside yourself. You have to be able to do it.

I can understand receiving as an important opening in relationships. I keep putting it there—from the outside coming in, as if someone else has to give it to me for me to receive it. That seems so limited.

It is. If the outside thing never happens, you will still have to have done this. As you know, the outside aspect has its limits—people change, and relationships are fluid.

Right. I am seeing a tiny seedling in my center, new and fragile. I will care for it and it will become robust and flower. What kind of plant is appropriate? My favorite flower is the iris. But that is seasonal. What about a flowering tree?

What about tending it and seeing what it becomes.

Oh, thank you. That has been helpful in so many areas of my life—no need to decide ahead of time. Put out the intention and decide in the moment, then see what manifests.

We so often look to someone (or something) outside of ourselves to fill our empty places. This conversation showed me how we are responsible for filling our own selves with Love:

I dreamt this morning that I was outside a mall somewhere. I noticed that I was standing next to two tough women, and they were semi-nude despite the cold weather. (We could see our breath.) They appeared to be prostitutes. They knew each other well, and one was constantly physical with the other—a mix of sexuality and roughness. We were kind of talking, and the one closest to me said, "*The only way to have Love is to make Love.*" I woke up right away, perplexed. There are many ways to take that. Women who are prostituting themselves (openly or unconsciously) may believe that the only way to be loved is to have sex. But this could also be a spiritual message. The closer woman (Tina Turner pretty) has just now turned to me and winked.

Here are some ideas about that quote: In order to have Love, you have to make it yourself. You can't "have" someone else's Love, you can only own what you have in yourself. Or, the best way to attract Love is to be creating Love yourself, to be what you what you are expect from the other person.

Tina is shaking her head No. Can you help me out here?

Well, honey, you can't go around expecting something that you don't have yourself. You need to be giving Love, not favors or things that you later resent. You gotta have this big golden well inside you that you replenish all the time, so you can be ready to give a big dose of Love and not feel emptied by that. When you get there, there will be so much Love inside you that you won't even need someone else's.

I have been thinking about that lately, about people who choose to be nuns and forgo physical relationships so they can be filled by Spirit. Initially, it seems like withholding a basic human need, but it also means you have more room for Spirit. It's not that you deny yourself—it's that you make room for more. Tina is nodding. And I wonder who you and your friend are, that you are here to teach me.

How you see us physically—this is how it is when all one can see is the physical side of Love, the hope of spiritual redemption in the physical world, reaching for a way that is not there.

I am doing that, by wishing for a lover. Realizing this, I feel a loneliness, the heaviness of having to accept what is. Yeah, I know that ultimately we are all alone. Come in alone, go out alone. I don't want that to keep me from having intimate relationships. How does filling my own self up with Love, with Life Force—how does that happen?

You gotta go where life force is and drink it in. You got to cultivate it, plant the seeds and tend 'em. You gotta stop being so picky about who you hang with. Check it all out. Be part of all of Life. Gotta take a look at fears, because that is what keeps you from experiencing Love even when it is right in front of you. Shutting down and drinking in can't go together. Some others push away instead of shut down—that doesn't work either. Got to be a balance, where you are all right in yourself. Be the Love. Not some hippie concept of la-la-la. Actually be present in every way.

What do I do to practice that?

Quit thinking so much, and just do it! Go grab life, get at the heart of it and feel that. Get offa this couch! Practice enjoying stuff! Dive in and swim! And you don't have to fuck to be sexual. Look at me and Lucette here. You thought we were 'hos. We're just two girlfriends doing what we like. Let go a little. Ha!

Tina is laughing with Lucette. Then she comes at me with her mouth open and swallows me. Instead of tumbling, I am head down and rotating. My head pops out of her ass. She shrieks and pushes me in. But I don't want to be in her shit hole, so I zoom out. I am about two inches tall. She is laughing. I sprout little fairy wings and fly up in her face. She is trying to catch me, laughing. I buzz up into the clouds. There are a lot of fairies up here in the clouds. Do any of them have shit on them, like I do? I feel ashamed, even though I have silvery sparkly wings just like them. There is a little shower of glittery water and I am rinsed off. Other fairies rub flower petals on me. I still feel like shit. It's where I came from. That is my real life, too, where I came from. If I was going to re-parent myself, what would I do? I would want to be hugged and loved up, told I was great, given affirmation for my feelings. And what am I doing now? Wishing for a lover to do that for me. I do hug and love up and praise others. I don't do it for myself very often. I need to Be the Love I want. Tina is pointing at me, like Right On. I don't accept praise or attention very well. But if I did start sucking up that Love, how would that be with Ego then?

57

You got to have that engine in good running order. You can have all the fuel you want but if you aren't tuned up you won't go. What good is that. You already know that you aren't more important than anybody else. But you are also just as important as everybody else. You are a star in the universe. Shine it up, girl! Be as bright as you can. Make some Light in the Universe. This little light of mine!
I'm gonna let it shine.
That's right. Now go have some fun!

What a journey. I feel that I am healing very old wounds, carried from generations long past. I have felt this before. Any words on that?
Universal Wisdom: *Women did lose their voice. It is one of the reasons that the planet is currently out of balance. Voice is not the only thing that needs to be recovered. There is also the sense of play and love, the beauties of childhood. Those are currently being devalued and discarded.*
We are too rational.
Too intellectual. Not enough heart, and not enough intuition.
Which is where we really connect with the Universe.
Connection can happen on all levels. We do not wish to throw away the mind. It is good to be thinking deeply. We want to balance that also with feeling and movement. Art, not because it needs to be analyzed, but because it is good exercise to do it.

After these discussions, I took a break and got involved in many social and community opportunities. Although I was not writing about them, my spiritual growth continued. **Universal Wisdom** invited me into a conversation about this when I returned:
You have been absent. You have had many experiences in that time. Talk about your shift.
I received an e-mail exploring the apparently invisible nature of mothering, how unappreciated mothers feel. The gist of the story was that my actions are not invisible—God sees them. I thought about this in terms of mothering but also in terms of all the pain

I was experiencing, especially the trauma I hold around the end of my marriage. When I see that I am never alone, that God is witnessing this pain, I feel a huge burden release. It's as if I thought I needed to hold that pain so that it could become visible, as if it was unseen. I have held onto it as if I could eventually hold someone else accountable for it. Acknowledging that God witnesses this pain reminds me that I am *not* alone with it. It moves me beyond the bubble of my pain into a greater context, where everyone has pain. It is part of living. I have always known this rationally, but this time I felt it spiritually.

When I think of God witnessing my pain, I can see the surface of the planet with people standing on it, each one with their own unique experiences, and with lots of space between each person. There is room for it all. It is what we are here for—to have experiences that feed back into The One With All. The learning is a process that adds to something else, something bigger. I want to come back to that. But first, I need to also note an observation about the nature of different kinds of energy transfer. Then I will step away and be the listener.

The other spiritual experience I had is related to the first one: I was responsible for coordinating a large cultural event. Afterwards, it was evident that this had been a positive experience for the community, and the effort I had put into it by me was appreciated. Others worked to convince me that I had earned the thank-you gift of a beautiful blanket. Although I had previously coveted that gift, I now felt very uncomfortable taking it. I put the box in my car. I could not take it into my home, so I drove around with it in my car for four or five days and listened to the gift. I could not give it back, because that would be disrespectful of the gift given to me. But then I had a realization—now that it was mine, I was free to give it away to someone else. I knew immediately who I would give it to. I brought the gift to this person and explained how it was moving through me, and I asked if she would please take it. She was very touched. We both cried. I felt *so* light, having listened to my heart and done the right thing. In the moment of giving and receiving, we were Moving Spirit. I knew that God was present in that moment, in that action. That movement of Spirit was an expression of God, a manifestation of God's Pure Love on Earth—just what we are meant to do. It was beautiful.

Later on, when I realized that God was also witnessing my pain, I came to compare the two experiences—standing alone with my pain and Moving Spirit. It seems that causing another to have pain, or carrying pain, is not a direct expression of God. Moving Spirit is. I wonder what there is to hear about this subject. I wonder about what it is that the experiences go back into, and whether or not negative actions are also an expression of God.

Universal Wisdom: *You are correct that your purpose is to experience God's Pure Love on Earth. We have talked about this before. There are many Beings in many dimensions processing this energy. Humans have physical presence as an added component in their process. (Yes, you are challenged right now to bring these concepts into words, because the concepts are much more complex than language.) Humans have the opportunity to use physical presence to create greater resonance when Moving Spirit. Moving Spirit creates a sensation in the body that is both created by and has effects on energy levels in the Universe. God is, very simplistically, the collection of these vibrations. Yes, they are occurring in other dimensions too, but that is not our discussion at this time. The sensation is not the goal, per se. The sensation is an indicator that Movement is occurring. One of the reasons we have talked so much about putting Ego in the correct position—in service to Spirit, is because that is the alignment that not only allows the sensation to be perceived, but also creates the circumstances under which Movement may occur.*

You are thinking about the biblical story of Adam and Eve, how they were given perception. This is a gift, the ability to sense the Movement of Spirit. It also creates a challenge, because other sensations can be distracting. It is not that sensation is negative. Many kinds of sensation are not only pleasurable but also add to the Movement of Spirit. We have talked before about the difference between pleasure and enjoyment. An example would be the use of food. Humans need to eat to survive. One kind of eating involves filling the body in an attempt to avoid strong feelings. Another kind of eating acknowledges that which is eaten—the joy and appreciation of a carrot grown in your garden or an animal harvested with respect. One serves the Ego, and the other Spirit. This is true of all *experiences.*

You talked about giving away the gift and how that Moved Spirit. The experience of negative events is not as easy to describe. This is because there are many facets to it. When someone chooses an action that harms another—and we will use the example of a conscious choice just to keep this simple—then both the person doing the harm and the person harmed have an opportunity. They each have the opportunity to recognize the action and address it in a way that moves spirit. This opportunity is present in all choices. Reaction is unskilled—it utilizes defensiveness or blaming or some other form of shutting down. This is not an environment for Moving Spirit. Moving Spirit utilizes True Compassion, which requires recognizing Self in the Other. It is a skill that is developed. Everyone is on their own path toward True Compassion.

To use your own example of carrying the pain—yes, it is difficult to look at ourselves, but that is how we improve our skills—initial harm was created by an unskilled choice. There were both conscious and unconscious elements to it, like most situations. Once the choice was made, each of you (and yes, the third party) had the opportunity to Move Spirit, to heal the harm of the choice. Each one made the effort they were capable of in that time. These efforts themselves were layers and layers of choices, as is all of Life. The parts that were not healed created more opportunities to Move Spirit. At some point, the initial action is covered by the layers of choices. It is never too late to go back to the initial choice. As you know, it is possible to heal harm created by those in past generations, even those who have passed on long ago, by taking compassionate action in the present.

A mistake you have made in this situation is your choice to freeze that harm in time, to not acknowledge the healing that has already occurred in this area. The healing may not be complete, and the harm can never be dissolved until it is fully healed, but one can choose a focus that also recognizes the beauty of healing. It is possible to fully heal without the input of the other doing the harm. It is a longer path. The one who has harmed another will always have the responsibility to heal that which they have created, but healing in the one hurt is not dependent on that. The harm itself creates a disruption to the Movement of Spirit. That is what is so distressing to the one harmed. What is most important to healing is the re-creation of the environment that allows Movement of Spirit. When you allow God to witness your pain, you are making Space for Movement.

Have compassion for yourself, and acknowledge that carrying the pain has inhibited Movement. Make choices that allow Spirit to move. Pay attention to those experiences. Continue to make choices that resonate in that way. Be responsible for your own healing. It is okay to be on the longer path. Remember that we are with you.

Thank you.

We are with you.

A Teacher came to help me increase my understanding around making these choices. **Mara** explains that the biggest choice we have is in focusing our perspective:

Today, my *hara*—my center, is a swirling gray funnel. I am moving into that vortex. There is a woman's face there, staring up at me. She is angry and snarling, her eyes flashing sometimes green and sometimes gray. She is testing me—sometimes she is nice, the next minute she is throwing the tea at me. She wears white chiffon. She has golden orange hair, pale skin, a long nose, and thin lips. She is pacing, talking. I say, "I'm ready," and wait. She is anxious, folding and unfolding her arms, wringing her hands. She seems unsure about talking to me. I would like to record your story, so it can be told again, save it from being forgotten.

My name is Mara. I would like to tell you something that is very old, something ancient. I am struggling to make it fit into the words and concepts of this time. It has to do with the beginning of the world, when the wind came. I am not comfortable in this body.

Can you be another form?

But then the emotions will not be as clear. I will try again.

My name is Mara the Malevolent. I was given this name through a misunderstanding. I am the waters of the Earth, the oceans. I have been marked as the taker of lives, because sometimes the sea rises up and swallows men. This was not always so. In the time before the wind, the waters lay calm. For the most part, they were solid. Solid ice. Everywhere. And there was a great cloud round the Earth that blanketed the sun. So there was nothing but cold. And in the cold there was ice. This lasted for a long time. A very long time indeed.

Then a terrible wind came. There is talk of where the wind came from, but no one was there to see it. They say that the wind came from the breath of God herself. And, of course, that would be true, because everything eventually comes from there. But there was something else besides. There was an accident where a burning planet hit the Earth. It was so hot, and the Earth was so cold, and the planet tore a hole in the clouds around the Earth. The sun came through that hole and began to warm the Earth. Then, don't you know, there was a difference in temperatures, with some places warm and some still very cold, and the wind rushed around trying to balance it all out again. The wind had good intentions—balance. But while the wind sailed around balancing everything, it also moved the air with it, and warm air circulated to places it had never been warm before, and things began to melt. The ice turned to liquid, to water, and began to flow and move. All of that movement helped itself, and before long you had ice moving, and water moving, and the wind lost control of its self, too. The whole thing was set into motion.

It is an injustice that I have but one name—malevolent. Malevolence implies intention. But I have no control over the waves. The wind blows and the waves rise up. Anyone who's out in 'em will have a rough time. Why are men out in 'em to begin with? Why to fish and feed themselves, of course. So you see that the seas are also full of gifts. And that is the way it is with all of the things that you see as negative. You have to be able to see a bigger picture to notice.

Gifts and danger are two sides of the same coin. You can't have a coin with only one side. There is always something on the other side. Turn your coin over. Don't always be expecting to take the gifts without receiving the risks as well. If all you see are the risks, without the gifts, well then that is your own doing, and you will suffer the risks only because that is what you choose to look at.

Another thing to know is that there are not just two sides. There is also an edge. You can hold your coin by the edge, so that you have both sides in the one hand. The edge appears small, much smaller than either side, but that is not the truth. Adding up all of the edge is also a significant amount, especially because it is easier to hold the edge than the side. When you hold to the edge, you can choose to let go, and let go you should. You should be spending your coin in this life, not hanging on to it, hoarding neither dangers nor gifts. The best gift is given, not received. Move your coin from your pocket to your hand, and then let go. If you must hold it, hold to the edge.

And what do you know of wealth? Wealth is not an external condition. You can't earn it with a million gifts. But you can earn it with a million loves. Hold your coin by the edge and let go. Make room for Love.

I seem to have lost connection. I was distracted by my own thoughts, and now this is fuzzy.

It's all right, then. You won't be needing much more of this.

I see that I can apply this to my situation. I look at the changes in my family and tend to focus on how my family was stolen from me, how I was beaten and broken because someone else couldn't own their problems, and I had trouble removing myself because I was tied to this situation through my children. Some days, I admit that I have also received gifts from this—growth, personal space, writing, and the chance to create a new family and a new life. Both sides are true. It is interesting to think of holding the edge of that coin. I can't see how to let go of it yet. I need to practice holding the edge, the balancing point where both things are the truth equally.

I hear the words from a Neil Young song: ".... like a coin that won't get tossed, rolling home to you." I see a coin rolling on its edge. Rolling home? Mara is nodding her head. I see the coin rolling right up to my chest, at once cleaving me in half and also melting me into a giant golden glow.

The supernova.

The coin melts and it drips molten, making me a shiny golden heart.

-3-

Traveling the Spirit Path

Although it may be hard to see sometimes, we always have choices. When we choose, we affect not only our own lives but also the lives of those around us. The following story was told to me by **Margarite**, a woman I've never met but who apparently used to live down the street from my grandmother:

It was very hard to live with that man. He didn't really care for me, you know. It seemed like he actually hated me. It started out that we just had different ways in the world. He went to work, and I kept the house. That's how it was then, for all us women. You didn't go out and earn money. There were no jobs for us. We were supposed to be home. And he was supposed to be working. And he lost his job. Lots of people did. It was the depression times. I imagine he felt bad about it, but he never talked. He just drank. And the longer that went on, the meaner he got. Hollering at me if something wasn't right. Pretty soon nothing was right. And it was all my fault. Because I was the only one that would put up with him. He just got meaner and meaner, swinging out at me, looking for reasons to hit me. I used to like to go up to the store, just to get out, but then I didn't want anyone seeing me all beat up like that, so I started staying home. And didn't you know I fell in a hole. A hole so deep that I couldn't see my way out of it. I began disappearing. Turning into the nothing that he claimed I was. Maybe he was right after all. He was stinking and dirty, and I didn't care what happened to me anymore, because there was just no way out of there at all. All I could see of me was what he saw. And he hated me.

There was a little house down the street, and they had two children. They just looked like the nicest children. I couldn't seem to have any children. I don't know why that was, but it was one more thing that made me worthless in the eyes of my husband. So I was there, in my kitchen, and that little girl came over for a visit. Came right up into my kitchen, where I was leaning over that sink with my hair all uncombed and my dress dirty. She was holding a plate in her hand with some bars on it and she asked me would I like to have some bars and could she please have one with me, too. Her mother had sent her over with them, and I think that on the way she decided that she'd like some of that too. She was just so clean and neat, in a little yellow dress, and she was as sweet and sunny as could be. Her name was Jeanie, and she must've been about five. I took my arms out of that soapy water and dried 'em off, and we sat down with a glass of milk each and had a little party.

That day just turned me around for the rest of my life. Every day after that I got up and combed my hair and washed up and straightened the house and went out to visit. If that little girl could see the good in life, well, I sure could too. I realized I had a choice about it. I didn't have to live a certain way just because my mean old husband chose that. I could choose something else for myself. I couldn't divorce, but I left him drink and cuss and snore, and I went on to have a fine life, with friends and everything. Because, you know, you get to choose.

There are always choices available to us. The four people in the above story (Margarite, her husband, my grandmother, and her daughter, Jeanie) all made choices that rippled out into others' lives. What we choose does make a difference. A well-known indigenous story summarizes this idea:

One evening, an old grandfather told his grandson about a battle that goes on inside people. He said, "My son, the battle is between two wolves inside us all. One is evil. It is anger, envy, jealousy, sorrow, regret, greed, arrogance, self-pity, guilt, resentment, inferiority, lies, false pride, superiority, and ego. The other is good. It is joy, peace, love, hope, serenity, humility, kindness, benevolence, empathy, generosity, truth, compassion, and faith."

The grandson thought about that for a minute and then asked his grandfather, "Which wolf wins?"

The old man simply replied, "The one you feed."

Both Jeanie's mother and her neighbor chose to turn and feed the good wolf. This is something that we are all capable of. The following conversation shows someone who chooses to feed the good wolf under extremely negative circumstances:

I see a petite black woman. Welcome, Grandmother. She has opened up her wide mouth, which is full of beautiful white teeth, and swallowed me headfirst. This is a process that brings the healing story into closer contact. I become it, and it becomes me. She takes me in and my cells feel it. Thank you, Grandmother.

I feel like I did at the Wounded Knee cemetery, my white skin on the outside, brown skin on the inside, the universe at the center of the layers. Today, I am brown-skinned. Dark, dark skin, beautiful chocolate. My arms are very skinny. My teeth are big and white, almost too much for my mouth.

Darfur Grandmother: *That is because I am so skinny. See how thin these arms are. My face is sunken too, and my teeth have no cheeks to comfort them. I am so thin, and I am so hungry. I can't remember what eating is like. There isn't any food. How can a body continue under these circumstances? It doesn't seem like this is possible. My brain is fuzzy. I feel like I am in a dream. The air is so thick it's hard to think.*

Where are you?

We are in Darfur. It is hot and dusty. It is dangerous. I have run so many times already. There is no safety. I have been raped many times. With this hunger, my woman-parts are hanging like elephant skin. I feel detached from my body. I am old, leaning on this stick, trying to sit in the shade. How can we live, with no food, no home, no safety? I wondered why they don't kill me. Why don't I just help them kill me? How is this living? But somewhere in me is the Light of Life. It is small, this little flame, but it won't go out. It knows how important it is to keep going, to keep this body going in the face of all the evil. We can't let the evil win, by going away. We have to keep the lights burning. Otherwise, who would be left when it's all over? My children are gone, I don't know where. My family is lost. There is just me. Stripped down to not even a body, really. But still a body. A house. A temple of the Light.

I am going to be alive when it's over, and then there will be someone to relight the fires. To touch the fires that have gone out, to shine for the other fires alone in their dark, to build back the bonfires of Love that will warm the earth. The core is everything. When everything else is taken away, the core remains. I let the evil ones see me as an old woman who can't fight. But they don't know where real power comes from. It's hidden in here, the center. It's where the stories are held. It's where Love is held and nurtured. They think I have nothing, but I am richer than they are. I have the universe, quietly simmering. That's my food, and I want to share a meal with you.

I am going to tell you something that you cannot understand just yet. You need to save this in your cook pot. Love it, stir it, and let it get the full flavor. You won't know what it means until you serve it up, share it with the soldiers. This is men's food. They are too busy to eat yet. The time will come, and you will serve them this meal:

Back in the days of the desert, there was only sand, red sand, and wind, and sky. The Earth was once this way. There were no footprints in the red sand. Only the wind walked there. The sun beat down and the sand was hot. The sand was made of grains, too many to count. The wind carried the grains around, creating mountains, valleys, and whirling sandstorms. The Earth was constantly being created and recreated. It was beautiful. The Great One enjoyed this peaceful creation. The sighing of the Great One made the wind. The joy of the Great One showed in the glowing sun. This is how the world was. The sighing wind sang the Earth's song. There was peace and there was joy.

This next part will become hard to understand. You are only the recorder now.

In the time of entra-e-in there was a change. It is sometimes said that the Great One grew tired of the sameness, but this is not true. The Great One changed what was being created. A new element was given to the world. There are stories about how the sand came to be. That is not this story. This is the story of water. Water was needed to balance the world. There was only the dry sand and the dry wind and the hot sun and the sky. Everything was burnt orange, and dry. The Old Ones tell of the time when water came. This story is in our bodies, because that is where we came from—the water. Our bodies know this story but we forget, because it was a long time ago and people do not listen like they once did. This is the story of where we came from.

The water came from Life. It came from outside the Earth. A big cloud entered the Earth's sky and wrapped around the Earth. It is a thing that happened. You will want to know where this could come from. People today want to know this kind of thing. People today want to own the information. But this is not that kind of knowing. It is awareness, which the mind receives but does not hold. This was the cloud of awareness. An energy cloud. It exists in the Universe. All things are possible there. All things. That is where the cloud of awareness came from. You can ask why, but that is not a question related to the cloud. When the cloud of awareness came, it covered the Earth with a quilt. The Earth went to sleep under the quilt, in the new darkness. The wind calmed, between the Earth and the cloud, and mixed the carried sand with wisps from the cloud. The Ground of Being swirled with awareness. In that swirl, the clouds thickened, and water drops formed. The drops became heavy and fell to the ground, and landed on the sand. Then some of the sand did not go with the wind, because it was heavy with water. Mud was created. The clouds and the sand continued to mix, and more drops were made, and fell to the Earth. Puddles formed on the mud, and then rivers, lakes, and oceans. The Great One saw that with the awareness had come compassion. First there was peace and joy. Then there was compassion: Understanding of Oneness, that all things are connected. Now the Earth and the wind and the sky were connected.

The Great One experienced this compassion. This experience of connectedness magnified Life Force, which is the energy of The Great One. Creation was then accelerated. The mud began to produce plants.

69

The Great One experienced growth, and Life Force was again magnified. The more Being there was on the Earth, the more connectedness there was. Connecting and compassion grew ever more Life Force. The plants grew, and animals came to eat the plants. The animals breathed the air and the plants breathed the air. Dependency one on another was created. Ever more connections, ever more compassion, ever more Life Force. The Earth was not just beautiful, but thriving. A pulsing, living cell, creating its own energy. A building block in the universe.

This went on for some time, so that the Universe also experienced growth, and the Earth, an energy cell, contributed to that. This was in the springtime of the Earth's existence.

It is important to understand this beginning, when the water came. Water is a mutable element. It changes shape with each contact it makes. It is its own self and it also becomes that which it touches. This is the way of compassion—to be one's self and also recognize one's self in the other. Compassion is evidence of Life Force.

I am telling you this because it needs to be known. We cannot have just the will of the wind and the heat of fire, a sterile environment. There has to be room for water to move, to join the Earth and the wind and the sky, to make the connections that will further Life Force. It is time for Earth and Water, for Love and Compassion.

Grandmother lays down with her stick. Resting, or gone? She waves me off. This has used much of her energy. Thank you, Grandmother.

I am interested in the importance of compassion, especially in regards to spiritual fuel. I will listen now.
Universal Wisdom: *As you have noticed in Ken Wilbur's writing,[5] there are three levels to everything.*
He calls it the I, the We, and the It.
Yes. This is one way to think of it, from a human standpoint. Actually, there are more levels than that, but this will suffice for our discussion. Compassion is a resonance, the deepest Love. Not pity, of course, but

---

5   *Sex, Ecology, Spirituality* (Boston: Shambala, 2000).

True Compassion, which comes out of the very dimension of Spirit. It is a connection on a universal level, recognizing the Oneness of All, removing any judgments which the ego likes to make to outline differences.

The ego needs to outline differences, to set its self apart. As it stands alone, it is poorly supported, so it uses judgments to explain why the object of comparison is less than perfect, making itself somewhat closer to perfection. This is nonsense, but Ego chooses not to see that. It is its nature, when acting alone, to choose the very drug of denial— isolation—which will be its downfall. When the ego is placed in its correct position, the Actor, it will mutually support the spirit, and the actions it takes will feed Spirit and thus support the entire being, in all of its concurrent states.

Compassion is one of the fuels of the spirit. It allows Spirit to travel on its soul path, which necessarily involves presence in several dimensions simultaneously. Compassion, as a feeling, feels good—there is a sense of well-being. Some describe it as heart-warming because it certainly moves one emotionally, to connect one's own feelings with those of another. But it also stirs the individual, the I, to understand itself in context, the We. It shows us, through these feelings, that we are connected to others, that we share certain experiences through feeling. It allows us to put ourselves in the other's situation and make a connection of understanding. Once we are able to sense the We through compassion, we also have the opportunity to put the We into a bigger context, to connect to Love, the vibration of Life Force that is timeless and unlimited. True compassion resonates on all of these levels. This is its purpose.

It is worth practicing compassion, to create resonance. Not in a sterile environment of cushion-sitting, but in active experience. Mother Teresa fully embodied compassion. The self does not disappear, because it is needed to coordinate the activities of compassion. Activity cannot be emphasized too much. Love is something you do. *Compassion is something you* do. *They can be thoughts and feelings, but part of the directive for human forms is to activate compassion. Activated compassion is fuel for spirit.*

I am beginning to put together the pieces, that Spirit also has multiple dimensions—I, We, It.

Yes. There are multiple dimensions. Wilbur uses a good description with nesting.

I had many questions the other day about just why this fuel is important to the All That Is. If the resonance moves in all directions, and there is a nesting factor, then humming up the individual spirit also hums up the other collectives, the We and the It and so on.

Correct.

Can you help me understand this in the context of *holons*[6]? The smallest items (the ants) are actually more important that the largest (the humans) because they support more Life Force. When I think of nesting, it seems like I would be at the center, with a bigger circle being the We and then the It. But how can the smallest be at the center?

It would be at the center of the individual's perspective.

Not being, of course, *the* center but *a* center, and the concentric circles of We run into each other and the It is all-inclusive.

Not really.

Okay. I'll be the listener again.

What you like to think of as concentric rings is really too limited, like seeing something as flat when really it is not. This is really about multidimensional presence. That some "thing" can exist in several dimensions simultaneously. A dimension is not a location. A dimension is an energy state—more like a quality.

Something like my brain can be a collection of chemicals and structures, and concurrently be my thoughts and also have the ability to time travel.

Yes. A rather primitive construct, but workable.

I suppose I am grasping after comprehension, but also a way to teach this.

Not really.

Okay, you're right—I am grasping at comprehension.

---

6   "Holon" is a term coined by Arthur Koestler: what is whole in one context is just a part of a whole in another context. In the infinite universe, nothing can be exclusively a part or a whole. Everything is simultaneously a part *and* a whole (a holon), and ultimately everything is connected to everything else by this part/whole relationship.

The minute you think you understand it rationally, it changes its quality.
But then how am I to teach this?
You're not. Sometimes this is just about deepening your awareness so you can move to another area.
I do feel like I am constantly expanding.
Yes, that is important—making room for more space.
What is in that space?
Other dimensions.
So I am only beginning.
Constantly.
Thanks for the temporal reminder.
As I sit here, my mind is moving toward my future. There are going to be some big tests for me, calls to action when I am used to primarily compassionate thought.
I am having the feeling of being Touched By God right now, only it is not so overwhelming this time.
You need to be able to live in that energy dimension.
It is like a settling and an aliveness both. Steady and totally free.
Try to maintain this state outside of writing. Notice it come and go.
Thank you.
Always.
Bless-ed Be.
Yes.

One of the teachers reminds us that in order to practice compassion, we need to break out of our comfort zone:
I would like to invite **Mrs. Rogers**, who has been waiting oh so long. I would understand if you had given up on me ever opening the door. I first met you (in this life that I know of) in a dream maybe twenty-five years ago. In the dream, I was in a country church with other black folk. We were having a choir practice. The church was empty and the choir was setting up to rehearse together in the front row. You invited me to come join the choir. I knew I wanted to sing, but I was afraid to join.

You are a petite woman, elderly in my contact with you, around seventy. You are black-skinned and well-dressed, the way older ladies do care about their appearance in public—a smart beige dress with matching short jacket, gloves and purse, a pillbox hat with attached mesh veil in the front. You have glasses, those Malcolm X kind like my grandparents wore. Maybe you were older when my grandparents were middle-aged?

Yes.

They were born around 1900, and they would have been middle-aged in the '50s. If you were seventy then, you could have been born around 1870 or 1880. Is there a date? No answer—it's not that important right now. You don't like all of these labels and descriptions of you.

I'm more than that.

Of course. I thought that this would help me reach back to find you.

Don't need to. I'm here.

Thank you. You have been extremely patient.

That's how it is for my people.

Constantly held back.

We perfected the kind of centering that you white folk are working so hard on now. Minor'ty people already have that. It is a survival tool.

It's a resource whites never acknowledge.

Racism does that.

Keep us from seeing.

Uh-huh.

I sense your impatience with me. I need to stop asking questions, jumping to conclusions and interrupting. I need to be a better listener. I will be still now.

There's a beginning to this, and no one really knows where it is. Back in the days of Jesus, there were many dark-skinned people. We all saw each other then, because we were looking at hearts, not skin. The sun shined on everyone. We had white places, and those were underneath, hidden by clothing. Private. Now whiteness is thrown up to be the holiest, and dark is what's evil. It's a sad state. Most of the world is dark. Can most of the world be bad?

Let me ask you—who is it that is using up all of the food and materials? Who is it that won't share? They are just feeding their greedy selves and killing the whole planet with them. It's crazy to think that anyone is against democracy. What we see is greed and selfishness and closing others out. That's not the way that man survived all of this time—by hoarding and fighting. There had to be some sharing and helping each other stay up, or the whole thing would've just collapsed. So all of this greed is against the laws of nature. It's just plain wrong.

And don't be thinking that it's not you. You sittin' ther' in your house watching TV and buying crap when you could be helping. Get up off your butt! There is work to be done, children. The beginning of it is to examine what it is you do and why you do it. "Just because" and "I don't know" are not answers. God did not put you on this green earth to keep your eyes shut. The minute you are born you got to be getting involved. You think that you are going to save yourself when the judgment day come, but you couldn't be more wrong. The minute it all starts coming apart, the left-outs are going to crawl over your walls and take you down. They are goin' to swarm like bees.

Your state of pro-tection is false. Look in the mirror. Do you see any one more human than anyone else? You do not deserve more. Unless you use your "more" in a responsible way—which means making it better for the people who have not. This is about a change in the whole way it works, the way it goes down every single day. If people hate you, then you got to help them feel like they are getting some. Getting some that feeds their bellies and heals their children, gives rest to their worries. The same as you want someone to be treating you.

You gotta be understanding the thing about Love. Real Love, which is not about making someone come over to your religion. That's a bunch of selfishness, not Love. You gotta take everyone and wrap them in your arms and make room for more. It can't hurt you, unless you don't do it. How do you think I know this? Because I have lived a long time, longer than you, and seen more than you can ever imagine. The devil is working everywhere. If you are sittin' on your butt and not getting involved, then the devil is working in you. And you know it. That is why you have no happiness in your life. That is why you are overweight and out of shape. You are sitting idle, which is the work of the devil. Yes, yes, you work until you wish you could die. But that is still idle, because you are not living through your heart. You are not living Love. You are letting your soul idle, when there is a lot of spirit work to be done. You know what I mean, and you know who you are.

What do I need to know?

Nuthin'. You don't need to know nuthin'. Because it's all in there already. Children know it. You have become blind to it.

It's hard for me to feel berated. You seem so angry.

Well, I am so angry. And you will just have to get used to it. Us minor'ty people have had to swallow it all back and it makes for bitterness. You white people don't want to hear that because it makes you feel guilty. Well, it should. It should make you feel guilty, not because you personally invented slavery, but because you aren't doin' a damn thing to change the injustice that exists now. You are just going along with a blind eye, saying there is nothing you can do. Which amounts to the same as inventing slavery. Because you are holding it in place, when you ought to be tearing it down.

You wonder why it is your responsibility, and I say that's because you got the power to do so and you are not using it. That is in your own best interest. Most of the people in the world are dark, not white, and when the fall comes, you will be few among many enemies. It's happening right now, and still you want to look away. You are making war where you have no business. It is stirring the bees. Only a few have been stung so far. You keep stirring, you will be overcome. It is almost too late already. You gotta leave the hive alone and give those bees some flowers to make honey with. Peace lilies.

Here's what you can start: have everyone in America who doesn't believe in the war adopt a family over there. Make connections. Help them regain their dignity and their lives. Direct messages, letters, apologies, I love yous. Make the innocent victims—everyday people like them and you—into real people. Say you're sorry. Ask how you can help. Tell them you don't support the war.

And another thing—we got to make a big deal out of that First Nation perspective. Honor the warrior, not the war. It's possible to be against the war and still support the soldiers. On both sides. Get involved with them. Say you're sorry. Say I love you. Real Love. Capital-L Love, not that sentimental romantic mush. The real thing, from the Soul. Ask how you can help them. This is called "Reach Out." That's the name of this operation. It's grassroots on both sides. By and to the people, not them government big shots. Although we need to include them, too, in forgiveness and love. But it has to start at the ground up. You are on the ground. Unless you are in that TV chair, and then you need to get up!

Wow. This is huge. I have been avoiding this?

You get on it, girl. Time is wasting.

Thank you so much. Thank you so much for waiting. I'm sorry, and I Love you.

Good night, honey.

See you next time.

I don't want to be seeing you until you been doin' somethin'. Kick your butt.

Mrs. Rogers wants us to take action. The Judge reminds us that *not* taking action also implies a choice, and has long-reaching effects:

Someone is pushing to get in. I will just be passive and listen and take notes.

Who is here tonight?

The voice of one you have heard before.

It is **The Judge**.

Yes, I have something to talk about that few people want to engage with. It is important to talk of war. To bring it home. Do The People really understand what is being done in their name? How can you wash your hands of it and go on, foolishly ordering another latte to go as if nothing is happening? The blood of others is on your hands, whether you pull the trigger or not. If you are not doing something to stop this, then you are participating in the slaughter. There is no neutral ground. Ignorance cannot be claimed.

This is true, yet I feel so powerless, and don't have any better ideas than anyone else around what to do with the situation.

You feel powerless because you can only hold the perspective that the military minds feed you. There is much more to the picture than this.

I recall Reach Out, which I have done nothing with yet.

Reach Out is a good grassroots idea and needs to be brought forward. There are other arrangements to be made. You must dismantle weapons as solution-makers. This is about a change in methods. Balancing power with women in leadership is a good start to this change. Women tend to diplomacy. The other thing is that babies need to be brought up in a culture of Love, not violence. No one is winning in the current culture. Yes, culture shift is a tedious task, but that is where it needs to start.

It still feels too big. How can I effect such huge changes?

Connecting with others is how it will happen. Connecting with others who are thinking these same thoughts.

I'm having trouble making this leap. I have finally found a niche where I think I can have some effect—public health work in a small community—the goals are distant but workable. Between that, parenting, and writing, I don't see taking on a whole new arena.

(I'm getting no response. I have defended myself right out of contact.)

There are many ways to be a warrior. It certainly can blend in with everything you do.

Then you are talking here about nonviolence in many arenas.

In every arena.

Everything I do starts with me.

You must have a strategy, a plan.

I am losing focus. What else do I need to hear?

Remember the idea of children laughing. That is what will save the world—children laughing. It's also important to laugh yourself. If there is no joy in what you do, it is not what you should be doing.

Mrs. Rogers and The Judge have been talking about taking action that relieves oppression. The following conversation puts oppression into an understandable context:

The topic I want to ask about is oppression. I want to learn about its origins and how it is perpetuated, what we can do to limit it. I would like to hear from a Teacher who can address this topic today. I see an older gentleman in a white lab coat. He looks something like Albert Einstein. He is pointing his finger at me, but not really looking at me. He appears flustered, or angry. I will listen.

The Doctor: This is not such an easy thing to talk about. We all think we know who is the oppressor and who is the oppressed. We think that someone else is the oppressor and that we are oppressed. We would all like this to be quite clear. Even though no one wants to be oppressed, and we are quite upset when we realize that we are, no one wants to be the oppressor, either. We so want this to be untrue that we are willing to deny that we are. But we are the oppressor.

You see, for there to be oppression, we all have to have the mental construct in place that oppression exists. We are sure that it exists, and when we see something that fits our definition, we say, "See, there it is!" When one tree falls on another in the woods, and knocks it over, do we call that oppression? Do we say that the wind is oppressing the trees?

Ah, but you are right to say that humans are not trees in the woods, and there is more involved than the wind pushing us around. But what is the wind—a gathering of energy. Sometimes it is a light breeze and sometimes it is a tornado. The Holocaust was a hurricane worse than Katrina. Where does this energy come from? In nature, it is created from the difference in pressure between hot and cold air. In human nature, there are also differences in pressure. Sometimes they are relatively benign. We would like to label these differences "good" and "evil," because this gives us a handy reference to use. But I do not like these names. They lead us to become judgmental. We are trying to be good, but actually behaving badly when we use judgments.

So I like to think of this in more scientific, neutral terms. Let us think of this in terms of positive and negative energies. Positive and negative relate to directions on a continuum. Something can be moving in a positive or negative direction in relation to something else. Therefore, positive and negative are not fixed qualities, but measured in relation to something else. We can say that the direction something moves has a positive or negative effect on something else.

In this case, the case of oppression, the positive or negative effect occurs not just on one individual, but on a group of individuals. The movement in one direction or the other is based on a fixed variable, such as skin color, or sex, or religious beliefs, or wealth. This should not be confused with suppression, where society places a value on certain traits, such as hard work, and attempts to control out those who do not fit this value. Suppression has evolution in mind, but is not always a positive direction. Evolution has a way of correcting out the mistakes it makes.

But, back to oppression. Check the dictionary.

There are two meanings listed: to dominate harshly, to inflict stress on. The key word I see is "dominate."

Yes. Oppression is about domination. People want to be in control of their world. They want everything to be the way they see it. They are uncomfortable shifting their view, so they ask others to shift in order to accommodate them. This is short-sighted, because people cannot change the fact that they are female, gay, black. It is foolish to think that these factors can be eliminated, that the world can be static. Change is happening all of the time. That is Life Force—constant change and renewal. It cannot be any other way.

We have gone through a long period where a few are dominating the many. You will notice in the definition above that oppression creates stress. Stress has an interesting presence in evolution. It will weed out those who are weak, and it will strengthen those who are strong. Within each variable (sex, color, etc.), there are some who are weak and some who are strong. An entire variable is unlikely to be wiped out. What remains are those within a variable who are strong. As long as they remain an individual variable, they will not have enough power to overthrow the dominating oppressors. Fragmentation strengthens oppression. What the oppressed need to see is their value in the whole, a whole which includes all of the oppressed as well as the oppressors. What the oppressors need to see is that they are a small part of the whole. Refer back to the Teacher who talked about the swarm of bees. When the shift comes, the oppressors will be overtaken by the swarm. Then there will be chaos. No one will "win."

What we all need to be aware of is whether we are making a positive or a negative shift. Are we fighting oppression with hate? That is a negative shift. Are we fighting oppression by creating links and raising awareness? That is a positive direction. Anything that moves energy in a negative direction is adding to the energy of the oppressor. It is helping to build up the bigger storm. Anything that moves energy in a positive direction is balancing out the energy of the oppressor.

Hating and blaming the oppressor is convenient—it gives the oppressed a target, a place to lay the blame. But rarely does the blame belong to individuals (except in some rare cases). It belongs to attitudes. Attitudes, meaning placation and accommodation in the face of un-truth, failing to recognize humanity in all beings. They lead to choices that feed the Ego at the expense of Spirit—greed, fear. Each individual has a responsibility to make choices based on Love. When the energy of Love reaches a higher level, then oppression will not have room to exist.

This takes action, too. We need responsible leaders, and that requires action. Get your attitude together and get up and move. Make room for peace and harmony. Sounds like a lot of love-child talk. But that is what it will take. Complaining has limited value. Name the wrong but then work to right it. Violence is a tool of the oppressor. Don't be tempted to put that in your hands. Do unto others—Live by the golden rule. Forgiveness. Compassion.

If you think these things are easy, you are wrong. They are much harder than picking up a weapon and shooting someone. Only the strong will manage to look at their own feelings and work through them. The oppressed have had these opportunities. Use them. Remember Mara's discussion of the two-sided coin: there is no gift without a loss and no loss without a gift. Strength and awareness can be the gifts in oppression. Hold to the edge of the coin. The world is black and white, yin and yang, dual and non-dual, positive and negative. Hold it all. Build spiritual strength.

I would like to thank you for teaching today.

Yes, of course.

May I ask your name?

Yes, you may ask.

Please, sir, what is your name?

You may call me "The Doctor."

Are you someone famous?

I suppose.

Do I know you?
Of course not. Just call me The Doctor. That will be fine for today.
(He is shooing me away. These are irritating questions.)

One thing that is required for oppression to exist is the idea that we are somehow different from each other. We are more the same than we are different. We all come from the same One:

Anyone want to talk?
Yeah. I will tell you something and it has to do with Life. You white people think you own the place, because you once owned people and that's how you got all this stuff you got now. It don't mean shit, because all of us black people, brown people, every people, we know we got something that you don't. We got our own selves, inside us, which doesn't have nuthin' to do with what a person's got on the outside. That's right. I am going to tell this story about it.
(My hands are black, and Star Sky Forever, the Universal Me, is open and expanding.)
What I want to tell has nuthin' to do with you or what you did to us or any other relationship like that. It's black without the white, black on its own and not a mirror relationship thing.
  Once there was the first human in the world, and that person was black. That's the way it came down. Those first people were dark-skinned and lived in the sun. They were really smart, because they had to survive in nature. Their society supported that. Stuff was in balance, man, and those people knew it. They knew they had to be centered and aware to make it. Spirituality was in them, at the core. They had to be nice to one another and help each other out. There wasn't this thing about everyone smashing someone else down.
  I see a human woman walking. She turns and looks at me. Each of her eyes is a spinning globe. Then the globes stop spinning and I fall into her pupils, the dark tunnel into her core. The core is filled with white light. Brilliant. I am consumed by it, and become the energy inside her. I can feel her walking again. I am with her. I am in the energy that she carries in her womb. I am everyone who

is someday to be born of her. I will go through the tunnel to the outside world, I am the baby she cares for. I will grow up to bear my own children. Finally, here I am in some time called 2007. I am her offspring.

Treatin' black people like shit is about rejecting your birthplace. It's all connected to dishonoring women. Racism will recede when women are in charge once again. Males will fight against this, because they are the most afraid of anybody, that they could go back and be lost. Get lost in the tunnel. That's why they treat women like objects now, because they know they need them but can't own their own fears. Men have a lot of work to do. That is whut's holding us back. Men, with all that struttin' and ego-izing. They're the ones got to be convinced to let Spirit fuel the world. Women already know this, but they go along with the man's world because they are so accommodating.

Men have to decide that they want more than power and control. They got to realize the greatness of bein' in charge. How they gonna go there? By being shown the way. Women already got this. They got to show the way. Not push it on men—that would just make those men push back. It's their nature. Women just got to carry on and be theirselves. Quit accommodating something that don't work. Don't have to be showy about it. Quiet works good, 'specially when all they're doin' is not playing those man games. Woman got to be herself. Then men will want to be that too. This change gonna take a long time. Role models is the only way it can happen, and that gonna take a long time. So that's why women and men are not matching up right now. It feels like somethin' is wrong, but really it's because something is right. Women going to have to give up something, too. Women going to have to do without. Going to change the way things work.

I can hear Bob Dylan's words, "Gonna change my way of thinking, find myself a different set of rules."

That's right. You gonna have to be self-directed about this. Is gonna change on a personal level long before it makes a world change. Do what's right. Do it right now.

I've seen you before. You are a young black woman with a sweet face and a big afro. Could you give me your name?

My name is everybody.

83

Works for me.

You white people are so stupid.

Yeah. I'm white on the outside. I'm Brown Being in the middle. And I'm the Universe inside me.

Crazy too.

I am just the typist. Thought your story might like an author on it.

Well, I don't.

Fine. Let me know if you change your mind.

Angela.

Thanks, Sister.

She has been sitting in the shade of an outdoor archway. I'm in the sun. She leaves the other way and walks into the sun on the other side. Her back still to me, she turns her head, smiling.

I'm gonna be seein' you again.

That's good. That's real good.

People who have experienced oppression carry a lot of pain with them from those experiences. Some of that pain comes from their ancestors, who also experienced the traumas of oppression. This intergenerational pain is transferred not only through cultural and parenting behaviors, but also in cellular memory. We can support people with this kind of pain by accepting it as it is:

I am standing right next to Healing Grandmother at the window of Unknowing. She is smiling peacefully. Short, slanting forehead, she is small, dark-haired, Puebla. I follow her gaze into the mist. I see aquamarine-colored triangles arranged in a circle, like the sun. The flat sides move counterclockwise. That is me, contrary. She nods quietly. The turquoise wheel can spin, or stop. I see drops of red blood coming out of a turquoise fin at about seven o'clock. The blood lands on imaginary ground in the mist, and a yellow flower sprouts there. The flower has a flat head like a sunflower, and it turns its face upward toward the sun. Then I am the flower, and the flower's face is my face. The stem is my body, the leaves are my arms. I am stretching and dancing in the sun. The sun feeds me. This is Nature's sun dance. I hear drumming, and the singing at the drums. As a flower, I wish for a heart—like the drum. I see humans with hearts, and their hearts are hurting.

Healing Grandmother: *There are generations of pain in each of those hearts. Pain that each person carries but may not recognize. When the drums beat, it wakes up the heart. It wakes up the pain too. Traditional dancing is a way to move the pain. To connect with the earth and ease the pain through. Dancing is also a time to celebrate, to practice being happy, get reacquainted with what that feels like. So there is a lot of emotion moving at this time. Drinking alcohol is a way to pretend we are happy when the pain comes. We can have some laughs, but we do not feel happiness. We make ourselves heavy by weighing down the pain with alcohol. The pain needs to move to be healed. Dancing can do this. Ill health is an expression of the pain. Chronic pain. Intergenerational pain.*

Be gentle with those who are carrying a load. They can only put it down when they are ready. All you can do is ask, "Are you ready to put down your load?" I hear you thinking about this. It is okay to say that you think the load is hurting them, but you cannot say that now is the time to put it down. When someone is ready to put down their load, or bits of it, they may need some support. Ask them who they want to help them. If it is you, you must examine whether you really want to give that support. Be honest. Don't take more than you can handle. Get some help. Usually, the help you need is very nearby. Do not be afraid to ask. As you have noted, you must stay in your center. This is the only way.

You are needed. In part, because you are willing, but also because you are not carrying the same pain. Some people will see you as "clean." We thank you for coming. You are on your soul path and our paths meet here. No, this is not your ego. This is the blood of brotherhood speaking. Humanity at its root. Do not second-guess that which is given to you. Accept your gifts graciously and use them wisely. Be ready in every moment. Give thanks. Go in peace.

Thank you, Grandmother.

That is all.

This same Healing Grandmother came to me again to help me understand my place in helping others heal themselves:

I was in a sleeping-dream with a healer, a native woman. She was healing my body. She was pulling energy up and out, putting it in the proper locations. I felt very dream-like—not mentally focused. At the end of the healing she gave me two hoops, undecorated, each one about a foot in diameter. She drifted away and I walked on. I came to an outcropping of rocks, and looking over the edge, I threw the hoops over. In a short while the healer came back, looking for her hoops. She was troubled that I didn't have them—they belonged to her ancestors. I had misunderstood, and didn't know I was supposed to keep them. I tried to look for them, but the scene over the edge of the rocks kept changing and I had no idea where the hoops had gone.

Although she remained silent and unblaming, I could see that she was distressed. I felt intense guilt at my lack of understanding and the loss of the hoops.

I awoke to several sensations. One was thrill and awe and gratitude for the healing of my body. Thank you, Grandmother. Overshadowed by this improvement, however, was the guilt and disappointment of losing the hoops. I remembered Mara's teaching about the edge of the coin—the gift, the danger, and the edge. I have been trying to hold the edge of this experience in order to manage my distress.

The day after this dream, a local church was holding "Seven Hours of Peace." Anyone was welcome to go and pray, light a candle, write a prayer—what a beautiful idea. I went during lunch and sat in meditation. During that time, I began to see many native spirits coming from the east, toward me. They were in a large group, brown shadows. I realized that I would go to work with Indian people, and accept whatever part I am given in that healing process. The people at the front of the group came to me one by one and entered the circle of my meditation. As more and more came forward, they formed a circle and began a traditional circle dance. At that moment, I realized that I was holding one of the lost hoops in my lap. One of the hoops is The People (the original people, who were here before Europeans). With this realization, I could see the Healing Grandmother clasp her hands together and smile—one of the hoops had been found! I felt a great sense of relief and enlightenment.

Thank you to all of the grandmothers and grandfathers, all of The People, for helping me on this journey.

I am thinking of the second hoop now. I have a sense that the loss of the hoops is related to the oppression of the native people by white culture. Healing Grandmother is smiling. So there are things that white culture has taken, at least two hoops, from The People. One of the hoops is The People—their relationship to each other in a cohesive, meaningful culture, the roots of their bodies in the land, their ability to support each other. I see boarding schools, the thieves of Good Living for the next generation. Is there another hoop about community in context?

Healing Grandmother: *Yes.*

About Place in the world, being smashed into a tiny location (like a reservation) without the surrounding support of traditional natural or human resources—in fact in direct conflict with mainstream American values. Before whites, at least there were other people on the land who had the same values of respect and stewardship. Now Natives are surrounded by a culture of greed and consumerism and status-seeking. There must be a struggle to maintain traditional culture against this backdrop, especially when the younger generation is caught with a foot in each world or, increasingly, no foot in either world. There must be a clash between isolation and assimilation, another concentric circle around The People. This is the other hoop. But what would it be called? It is a disharmony. Can anyone talk to me about this?

Yes. This you will come to know, because some will want to blame you for it. You must let them blame you. Not take the blame, but understand where it comes from. You can show some that your heart is gentle and Loving. It will take a long time to trust. Some pain will be caused, but you must continue Loving.

(Former President Jimmy Carter has said that you must love God and also love whoever happens to be standing in front of you right now.)

You will be challenged. This is part of the process. Do not be discouraged. Reach for greater understanding. You are to be a bridge. You can hold a foot in each world. You must be strong. Many will not want to see this happen. You need not be a warrior. But you must hold your own faith. Quietly.

I can see that reserve, quiet, will be a needed skill. I am afraid of being unskilled.

Skills develop through practice. Be kind to yourself and others who are practicing.

Anything else today?

You are to be a community support. This is the other lost hoop. You do not make The People. That is their own job. You are the community around, which provides the supportive environment. One who heals scars from outside the community. Have faith in your purpose. Do not be distracted by details. Your path is certain.

I see it. It is a narrow track through the bush, but it is well-packed, like a portage trail.

Be ready to laugh. Humor will keep you whole.

Thank you so much. It feels right to have such a purpose. The stress of daily life falls away in the context of purpose.

Yet daily life is where the purpose is applied. The journey is one step at a time.

I have wondered where my family fits into this, especially my children.

They will grow rich from watching you. Include them in your journey.

Where does the book project fit into this purpose?

This is an important question. The book lays the foundation for the white world to understand, to gain perspective. It puts you in a position to make connections.

I do need to address some self-doubt. Vine Deloria, Jr., has written about white people trying to piece together their shattered identities by writing spiritual travelogues. When I read that, I felt flung into doubt. What am I am doing with this writing project— "bringing the ancient to the surface," as I was told. Is that real? Am I just letting my ego jack around my psyche?

Vine Deloria, Jr., has a perspective which you must be aware of. Do not swallow every word as belonging to all. Judgment is a negative extension of perspective. Know the difference.

Thank you so much. Bless-ed be. Is there a Native term?

Go In Peace.

The Teachers helped me see opportunities to further my healing. There are many opportunities for everyone:

I have been hearing that there is a lot of energy coming in now, as we prepare to evolve to the next level. I am very intrigued by that. It sounds like there are many centers for change. What about this would be good for me to understand?

Universal Wisdom: *It is like a spring welling up from the ground. Many places at once. Beautiful water to drink, some may feel like drowning.*

Where does it come from?

From the Universe. From inside, from everything.

This is unknowable to me.

In this manifestation, yes.

I'm feeling lost about where to go now.

Then just type.

Okay.

We were once better people. People lived in harmony with the land and each other. There was balance. We started to come out of balance when we became intellectual. There is a lot of head-stuck behavior now. The West has glorified intellect at the expense of the body and the soul. We are using our heads to justify more greed, disguised as development. The church contributes to this also, by shaming the body. All of this is why the Earth is in such poor condition right now. The Earth is not just a ball of rocks and dirt and water. Earth is an energy state. It is a body, of sorts. It requires balance, just as we do.

Just as our bodies do.

Yes. Think about the size of the Universe. And the Earth is one cell in that body.

Is there some way to make this more understandable, more basic?

The Earth is an energy state. It is made up of a collective of energies. The most important energy is Life Force, or Love. That is what drives plants to grow, clouds to form, babies to smile. Thich Nhat Hanh explains well the interconnectedness of all of this energy.[7] We really are all One. We are all related. Balance is needed so that all grows well. Beauty is a feeding force. Not that we need to make beauty. But we need to allow it. When we experience beauty in the natural world, we are experiencing the feeling of knowing what Earth is supposed to be like. We sense the seed of the soul—harmony. True beauty brings us home.

We are destroying this bits and pieces at a time. We don't grasp the situation as a whole. We want to believe that our contributions don't really add that much to the downfall. Our goal is to return to the seed of the soul. Not to go there and stay there, but to understand that it has to be the seat of choice and action. Spirit is the fluid expression of that. It is movement rooted in the seat of the soul. We need to get the world back in balance.

Is that why women are emerging as world leaders now?

It's part of it. Environmental work is there too. So is social justice. Church tends to be a wet blanket on the process because it is too often action done through the lens of trying to get others to be like you. It's not about accepting dogma and labels. It's about True Love. It's about meeting on Common Ground. It's honoring Fertile Earth. It's sharing the harvest among many. It's about resting in each other's company. It meets the needs of the soul, not the ego. It's done because it feels right, because it's the right thing. It's anonymous. It's clean. It does not leave damage in its wake, which Ego does. It's not exclusive. It invites all. It's not a religion. It's a way of Being. It's not a wish or a prayer, it is action. There is no fear or pride in it, no anger or misunderstanding. There is openness. It is a flowing. Imbalance creates blocks. Blocks create knots and tension and irritation, then blaming. Untie the knots.

I think about my own little microcosm, my difficulty letting go of another's betrayal behavior and their denial of damage. It's hard!

---

7   *No Death, No Fear* (New York: Riverhead Books, 2002)

Yes it is, and you are holding on to the damage like a prize. Untie more knots. Let them experience the consequences of their choices in a way that they cannot blame on you.

Sounds like I need a cleansing ritual.

The ritual makes the shift. It allows the shift to start so that energy can flow a new way. The new way requires practice, which can be built on the energy memory of the ritual.

Any ideas about ritual for this bigger shift in consciousness?

Get together with other people who are making shifts.

Like peace rallies?

That's one.

Is there something I can start?

Work on Reach Out. Things will shift.

I feel so overwhelmed by that directive. It seems so huge.

Because you have not started. It's like this project. Start with small steps. They will add to each other, and you will be moving easily.

I see the goal, somewhat, and a big blank in between.

Yes. It's okay to remember the goal, but focus on the steps before you. If you trust, if you are choosing right action, the steps will lay themselves out to you.

And a reminder to me to not get tangled up in personal relationships unless it really is about shared path.

Just don't get tangled, even in Right Path.

Oh, right. Tangles lead to knots.

Can.

This is not my focus now.

Don't eliminate it. Be open to all kinds of relationships. Sometimes something turns where you don't expect it.

Stay focused, stay open, lots of juggling.

No. No juggling. Right Attention.

Ask not what center can do for you, but what you can do for center.

That is supposed to be funny.

It seems that humor is not part of Universal Wisdom.

Humor is cultural, contextual. Universe is bigger.

Right. I'm getting this picture of Spock, in the 1960's TV series *Star Trek.*

They tried to use him to convey Universe. He was bigger than intellect, expanded into mind-space. That is not what is being advocated here, ultra-intellectualism.

What about the mind-space part.

Yes. But include the realm of the Unknowable.

Like faith, trust in the Universe.

Yes. And other experiences which we have not gotten to yet.

What else here.

You have to be listening all the time.

To Universal Wisdom.

To Universal Wisdom, also to others.

Because not everyone is going to speak the same language on these matters.

Because people have other ideas. They are all pieces of the whole. It all needs to get pulled together.

Linked.

An arm-in-arm link. Not against something, but as a celebration.

A visible, energy-magnifying celebration.

So others see this and want to share it too.

This is a movement.

It is drops joining into waves and waves joining into a sea shift.

I'm thinking of global warming melting the ice caps.

It is part of the energy being released, attempting balance. Humans see that as catastrophic, and many changes will be made, but it is about returning to balance. There cannot be harmony and imbalance at the same time.

So don't get all wigged out about climate change, use it as a call to harmony.

Others are working on the climate change. One of the many centers.

Like the feminization of political leadership.

That's another. Link Arms.

Wow, there's a cool logo: Link Arms to Peace, and it shows open arms connected, with each body a link to Peace (personal, community, habitat, cultures, ecosystems, planet).

Use that.

I'm feeling the need for some clarification. On what my part is. It's not eco or political per se.

No. It's about social change.

What I have been connected to---gender issues, people's stories.

Yes. It's about social connections between people.

Thank you. That's helpful.

The other components are important too, linking it all.

That's about the listening to others, as you said above. Pieces of the whole.

Yes.

This is feeling like enough for today.

It can be.

Is there more.

There is always more. You have tired.

Yes.

Then it is better to wait.

Thank you so much. Every time, thank you. In between times, I get to feeling lonely and isolated and scared and a little crazy. Then I come here and it falls together. This makes so much sense. It gives me faith.

You need to bring that faith into the "real" world. Remember that you never go home alone---you always have yourself. Keep praying your spiritual life into existence.

-4-

Experiencing Space

I had been thinking about some of my Teachers' main discussion points—Ego, compassion, oppression—when I realized that compassion and oppression are two sides of the same coin. The edge of the coin may be the ego, and the side displayed depends on the position of the ego. What more can you say about this?

Universal Wisdom: Yes. The position of the ego is an important point. It is some of the thread that weaves these lessons together. But there is more to it than this. There are some threads that are moving into place that will illuminate the transcendent nature of Spirit. Spirit wants to transcend—that is its purpose. Transcending fulfills its purpose. Many humans sense that their physical beings want to expand. They have been crushed into a small space by cultural learning. What they want is more space. They want to expand and allow more energy to enter the space between matter. This is only possible with transcendence. Yes, the language will be difficult for the average person. You are practicing it right now.

Expanding my energy beyond my physical body. It's part of what allows this information into my mind space.

Yes. The average person can practice by increasing their awareness of space around them.

There is an exercise that I find helpful, one that involves placing my attention in space, increasing my space awareness, looking for and finding it in smaller places and greater amounts all around me:

A good place to start is in the forest. Sit still and center yourself. Quietly notice all of the space above the trees. Then add all of the space between the trees to your awareness. Add the space between each twig on each tree, and all of the space between each of the leaves. Then recognize all of the space that is under the tree bark, between each blade of grass on the ground, between the hairs on the back of a buzzing fly. Keep adding. Really look. Become aware of all the space that exists everywhere. Keep looking and realize that there is much more space than matter.

In a city, stop and look above the buildings, look at all of the sky. Then recognize the space between the buildings, acknowledge the space in the rooms *in* the buildings, between the people on the street, between the cracks in the sidewalks, under a pebble, under your foot. Add all of the space together at once and allow your awareness to rest there.

In a house, become aware of the space in all the rooms, under the table, under the chairs, under the bed, between the sheets on the bed, between the threads of fiber weaving the sheets together. On and on and on.

Keep expanding your awareness. Look at your own body and know that there is space between your body and your clothes, between each hair on your head, inside your nose, inside your lungs, inside each cell in your blood, between the atoms in the molecules in your blood.

Keep looking and becoming aware of space. Gently hold all of the space at once until you see that all of the space is continuous—it is all connected. Eventually, it will become clear that collective space is limitless.

It is something that has to be experienced and practiced, not just thought about. This kind of attention is used to increase awareness of the space, of the not-matter.

Shifting one's attention to Space can be challenging, because Western culture immerses us in a worldview that is Time-oriented. Time orientation focuses on objects and uses the clock to measure all events. It places things one after another in an orderly fashion. Linear organization—jumping from one object or point in time to the next, also encourages the development of hierarchies to explain the relationship of one person or thing to another. These linear arrangements are visible in top-down cultural institutions like government, organized religion, and patriarchal families. Hierarchies function with fixed rules about how things came to be and how they will stay that way. They force reality to "stay in line." Many people are comforted by the apparent stability that linear thinking offers.

Westerners are focused on Time, however, at the expense of our awareness of Space. Space is the environment where we exist. It is *not* neatly ordered, because it contains everything at once. The space we end up ignoring when we focus exclusively on Time includes our own bodies, as well as our relationships with other people on the planet and with the planet itself. This is evident in our appallingly poor health as a nation, our attempts to ignore the world's poor, and our resistance against taking responsibility for climate change. We end up valuing the hierarchies of status and ownership, creating a celebrity and consumer culture.

What would spatial orientation look like? We have many examples available, although we discount them precisely because we don't understand them. Indigenous worldview is Space-oriented. In indigenous cultures, there is room for Time, but it is not linear time. It is cyclical time, seen in the turning of seasons and life cycles—and all of the cycles connecting endlessly to each other. This nonlinear thinking sees everything as connected. It encourages honoring and sharing and stewardship. Not rules and hierarchies, but relationships and shared community are valued.

Culture that is Space-oriented connects not only people but also place. The place where things happen is important because of what has happened there. People gather and honor these places because that practice invites communication with the spiritual world. Relationships between humans and plants and animals and the land are inclusive spatial connections. They have spiritual value. The clock is just a piece of machinery.

Anyone who has traveled in the third world knows the frustration of scheduled transportation there. This frustration is due to our layering of linear thinking over cultures that are spatially oriented. We stand and look at our watch, fuming because the bus is two hours late. We assume that because the schedule said that the bus would leave at a certain time, it will. But in a spatially oriented culture, the schedule is only a piece of paper. The bus will leave when it is ready. It will leave when there are enough passengers who want to go. The bus will leave when the driver gets there. The driver had to stop at his grandmother's house to pick up a package, and now she has invited him in for something to eat, and he will go to the bus stop when he is done with that. The exact time that the bus leaves is not important. Cultivating relationships in the community is.

Much of the ancient teaching that is now being brought to the surface is about honoring Space rather than Time. I am intrigued to make these shifts that improve well-being. Well Being.

I am being encouraged by a male elder to write. Every time I start to ask a question, he motions toward the laptop. So, I am to listen. He nods his head. He wears a southwestern shirt, pants, and vest. A scarf is wrapped around his head. He is dark, wrinkled, indigenous.

Indian Grandfather: *When you were coming in to the world, we were going out. Our people had been killed and beaten, scattered. There was very little hope then. The whites had come and taken our ways. This is the foundation of both the white and the Indian people who are living today.*

Who would you be if someone had come and burned all of your churches and Bibles, and killed the men of the church and forbidden your religion? This is what happened to the Indian people, but not in the way you think. The Indian Spirit is carried in the land and in the hearts and blood of the Indian people. We were pushed off the land of our grandfathers and grandmothers, the land that holds the link to spiritual experience. These were our churches. The stories that connected our people with the Spirit World, which taught our children and made our way in the world, these are carried in the hearts and blood of our people. Our people are our Bibles. All of this was destroyed in the way that the whites treated us. We did not know how to fight back because we did not understand how the whites saw the world. Now we know. And as we rebuild our Life Ways, we keep that to ourselves. We cannot afford to have whites get a hold of this again. It is our source, our center. It is vital to our existence.

You will not see this for many years. You must be trusted first. You will still be learning. You are being groomed in the Dream World. Continue to pay attention to the Dream World. Carry those messages through into your daily life. Live out the dreams. Take the hand that is offered to you. Understand that dreaming is Life, it is not separate. Let go of the boundaries of time. Some things will not make sense when they are in order. Hold all of the pieces together. Be gentle.

Grandfather has his arms folded and is looking away. We are done. (He nods once.)

I do have questions for the Universe. I am confused about how this information fits together.

Universal Wisdom: *You don't have to be. Quit second-guessing everything. Just go with it. Do you feel you are doing the wrong thing?*

No. I wonder if I am sidetracked, not meeting my obligations.

What obligations?

To produce this book.

It is not about producing. It is about Living.

Giving up the linear track.

Experiencing Space. Things will happen when it is time for them to happen. If they are out of order it is because they are out of order. You can't paint an entire canvas with one brushstroke. You can't play a symphony with only one note.

Nonlinear.

Not-time. Practice qualities, not quantities.

A series of conversations and guided visions followed, which helped me to understand the relationship between Time and the experience of Universal Space right inside my own body:

Who is here today? I see Ronnie Wall's face looking out the window. I'm wondering if he should speak, and he's a little irritated by me saying that. Mama Africa has gotten up and walked out of my vision. So I am not approaching this correctly. I will sit quietly and meditate, relax, not be so pushy.

I am watching a fish swim up from the lower left of my vision. I am following it from above, watching its body movements, the easy swish and bend of its body, the flow through the water. Now I am seeing it from the side, especially the mouth, the lips opening and closing. Now it is facing me head-on.

Fish: *I have something to say.*

I am listening.

I need to say that there is a world of which you are unaware. You will be entering this realm by following me. Just describe what you see.

This is like a dream. All around the fish is white light, with no other context. I cannot see the water, but I feel it, an awareness of flow. I am behind this fish, just behind the dorsal fin. I am hearing the shaman's words about time being a fish and we are on the back of the fish for a while, and then we fall off.[8] I am on the back of the fish, holding onto the fin in the stream. We are swimming through white light and clear water. The fish is effortlessly pulling me along. It is a pleasant sensation. Drifting. Flowing. Occasional bumps and jerks. Now we are picking up speed, faster and faster. I am holding on tightly, a great wind rushing by. I have to put my head down

---

8   The quote from *The Last Report on the Miracles at Little No Horse* by Louise Erdrich (Perennial, 2001):

"Time is a fish," said Nanapush slowly, "and all of us are living on the rib of its fin."

Damien stared at him in quizzical fascination and asked what type of fish.

"A moving fish that never stops. Sometimes in swimming through the weeds one or another of us will be shaken off time's fin."

"Into the water?" asked Damien.

"No," said Nanapush, "into something else called not time."

a little. We are going faster and faster and faster, as if to break an energy barrier. The wind is howling in my ears, and I am holding on with both hands. The energy vibration is rising higher and higher. Everything is a blur, even the fish. Like centrifugal force, I feel my own energy being pushed down my body and off of my feet. I am aware of my feet. I have brought my legs in tight around the fish's body like I am riding a horse, in order to stay on. My hands are gripping the fin, my head down to protect my face and my hair streaming back. Energy is roaring by. And then we pop through a surface. There's a sudden calm and stillness. The fish just floats lazily on top of the water, and I am looking around at a beautiful landscape—mountains in the distance, forest at the shore, blue sky, birds singing. The sun is shining down. It is warm, and the water is full of sparkles. An occasional cool breeze ripples the surface. The fish slowly submerges, and I remain at the surface, buoyed by the sparkles. The surface tension of the water is enough to hold me up, and I am rolling in the sparkles. They stick to me like stars. I am like cotton candy being made, but I am collecting star sparkles. The sparkle water is a healing bath. I am letting the sparkles sink into my body through my skin, through my muscles. They have joined with the infinite sky inside me— the universe inside me that is Star Sky Forever. I am enjoying the pulsing of that vibration. It is the pulse of Life. I see that this Sparkle Lake is the bowl of my pelvis. There's a new reality there. During the last year, that reality had the appearance of the grass of the pow-wow grounds, with children in grass-dance regalia poking their smiling faces into my view. Lately, I have been able to conjure the vision but not the sensation. Now the Sparkle Lake is there. The Sparkle Lake is inside my pelvis and, simultaneously, I am a being on that lake. I see myself jumping into the lake, doing a cannonball, and the waves splash sparkles all over my insides. The fish is in the lake, tickling the lake bottom and me. My heart is the sun, shining down and creating the sparkles. When I breathe, the breeze ripples the lake. The forest and the mountains, my body, are the shore. Who are those birds that I hear singing? That is my Spirit. What a beautiful vision! Thank you, fish! When I breathe into my center, into my *hara*, it is a long breath. It pushes away the water and I can see the muddy bottom of the lake, the little plants growing there. The water parts in a funnel shape, and a hole opens up in the lake bottom. Through that hole I can see down to the world outside my body. What is that hole?

Universal Wisdom: *It is your connection to the outside world.*

That is what we seek through sex—a connection to the infinite universe in another. Which is why I have to wait for the right other—the connection doesn't happen with another who is not open to their own universe.

Yes.

I am thinking of other places of connection. My fingertips are next. I see rainbows on them, rainbow swirls that are all over my skin but very concentrated on my fingers. Rainbows are something to share and blend. They are illuminated by my heart—the sun. Heart warmth can be felt, too. Birds singing Spirit Talk is something that can be heard. These are the senses— Spirit in action, communication, communion. I don't think it is just a coincidence that it is spring now in nature. I am being given the gift of a birth day, the birth of physical Spirit. Most of my life, I have been challenged by the need to feed my physical body, and I have not been making the connection of physical spirit.

You left there as a child, in a response to danger. Come home now.

Tears can fill the Sparkle Lake, but so can melting snow, the thawing of frozen states of being. Food is a gift offered to the temple. Rest is the balance of night. Compassion is the warmth of the heart-sun. Relationships feed it. I have just reached out and stretched. The air around me is geometrically shape-shifting like in an acid trip. Dimensions in motion. I want to stay here forever. I also have to function on this physical plane.

You can stay here. You will need practice to maintain it. This vision is a gift, a prayer book to open when you are getting lost.

I see fish swimming up and down inside my arms. Fish are swimming inside my skull. What is my meditative mind?

Your brain is a sense organ. Your mind is God.

And my spine?

It is the conduit between center and God.

Sitting in a chair all day silences center, dulls it. That is why I am so tired at the end of the workday.

Yes. Legs are the tree roots, sucking up moisture and nutrients from the earth. Walking keeps them supple and alive.

I am so lucky!

Yes, you are. Feel blessed.

Bless-ed Be.

Blessed be.

Who is the fish?

That is another day.

Always more mystery to look forward to. I'm smiling.

Is there anything I need to know before I sign out?

You will be tempted to share this right away, but you are not ready. Reporting, using words, will dampen this effect. Enjoy the sensations and the vision. Get comfortable with the feelings before you talk about it. This is both sensual and spiritual. Live there. Practice. Be Love.

Be Love. Bless-ed Be.

Blessed be.

Big Thanks.

There is a connection between Sparkle Lake and the quote from Louise Erdrich's book—the fish. A fish came and spoke to me through our minds, taking me on the journey into Sparkle Lake, the expansive world within my own body. As part of the awakening of my physical body, I see similar fish of pale silver-gray swimming in my body. I especially see them in my arms when I hold them out to fill them during my energy practice. They swim swiftly back and forth, up and down my arms. There is some connection. I asked at the end of the Sparkle Lake meditation, and I was told, "Not today." Could I ask that today? What are these fish in my body?

Universal Wisdom: *Yes, the fish are Time. Time is inside you, held in the places that store memory. The fish travel back and forth communicating information.*

Can I ask the fish to bring certain stories or information to the surface?

No. The fish are operating as fish, as Time. They are in motion and do not answer requests.

Then Sparkle Lake was an open window, an opportunity?

The Sparkle Lake meditation prepared the foundation for Seeing, creating support.

I see that. Is there anything else I should know about the fish?

They are not always so visible. This is a dimension you are not yet ready for.

I often react with some frustration to that limit. I also understand that this is a layered process. I accept the wisdom of unfolding and the unfolding of wisdom. Is there a whole topic area I am missing in the writing?

Yes.

I just heard the word Time in my mind, and also the words of Thoreau: "Time is but the stream I go a'fishing in."[9]

Time is a big area that is little understood.

And time is somehow related to the fish in my bloodstream.

Time is an energy.

Which is manipulated by our attitude.

Partly.

Time is an energy. Tell me more, please.

Time is fascinating to humans. Humans think that Time is a fixed quality. It is not. Time is fluid and changeable. Humans need to fix Time in order to stabilize their reality. This has the effect of making things appear linear. People who live outside of modern technology know that Time is nonlinear. Time is a universe which contains everything at once.

I see the fish in my bloodstream, swimming back and forth, carrying information, connecting.

Those fish are what make it possible for you to access cellular memory. They travel between one cell and the next, making connections through contact. Nanapush was correct, that you are riding on the fin of a fish.

---

9   "Time is but the stream I go a'fishing in. I drink at it; but while I drink I see the sandy bottom and detect how shallow it is. Its thin current slides away, but eternity remains. I would drink deeper; fish in the sky, whose bottom is pebbly with stars. I cannot count one. I know not the first letter of the alphabet. I have always been regretting that I was not as wise as the day I was born."

You think that your life is about traveling from one point to the next, but that is only the section that current awareness allows. You can be on that fin for a very long time.

If time is energy, then the thing that is not-time is called what?

It is called movement, and you are not ready for this yet.

Excuse me for interrupting. I am the listener again.

Good. It is important to understand the nonlinear nature of Time. That will help you as you travel in other dimensions. You understand how healing the present extends healing into the past and the future. That may be perceived as linear—past to present to future. But it is not, because the past, present, and future all exist simultaneously. They are not separate. And the past, present, and future that you see on the continuum of your own life is actually connected to the web of we-are-all-related. So everyone's past and present and future all exist simultaneously and are all connected to each other. And that is what Time is, not a captured tick on the clock.

I sense an understanding of this. I wonder if there is an example that could make this more concrete, or a description or metaphor.

The explanation is the example. The metaphor is the fish, of course. And each person is not holding on to the fin of a fish, of their own fish. It is the experiences of humans that are on the fin of the fish. The experiences create information in the form of energy, which is then transferred to all of the other experiences. When you access the information, you are entering the dimension of nonlinear time. That is why you can hear stories from the past. It is the resonance of the experience that is transferred in the information.

Resonance, vibration.

There are certain resonances that add to each other to create new development, what you call evolution.

But "evolution" is supposedly locked in linear time.

Yes. New development is a result of resonance at certain harmonic levels.

What some people call "humming up."

Yes.

Lately, it appears clearer to me that *Grandmother Dreams* can add to the humming.

Yes. It is all additive. You are wondering about the change coming. The change will come from many directions. Some of them will appear traumatic, in the context of linear time. But the end effect will be an opportunity for a new resonance, a resonance that can permanently alter the function of the cellular level, making new things possible in nonlinear time.

(I was just feeling a little overwhelmed, found myself running my fingers around in a circle over my third eye, in the middle of my forehead. I placed a finger in the center and pressed, and I felt energy ripple through my brain from front to back.)

These are some of the places where change will evidence—in the third eye, and the ability of humans to see into other dimensions.

I have been blessed with a great gift, and fall humble in that presence.

Some have to go first. Remember the two sides of the coin.

Yes. A loss will come too.

Do not be discouraged by this. Hold to the edge.

I suddenly feel very sad, and I don't know why.

This is the awareness of loss.

What have I lost?

Your innocence. The ability to function securely in linear time.

Balanced by the gift of nonlinear travel.

The edge is a foot in both worlds, both linear and nonlinear.

This is what Healing Grandmother spoke to me about—being a bridge.

Which means you will have acceptance in both areas and rejection in both areas.

Which is why I was instructed to hold to the center, to faith. Thank you for your compassion.

You are never alone.

I feel an incredible intensity. I am crying. I feel that I am in the presence of God.

God: *You will know me through the resonance.*

Why am I crying?

A powerful connection is being made.

106

Yes, I am overwhelmed. I am hyperventilating. My whole body, every piece and cell, is lightweight—as if it is becoming an exploded view and there is light in every space between. The white light in the spaces is denser than the once-connected cells. And now I feel peaceful and rested, although my mind is unfocused. My whole self is expanded. This is the White Light of God. I feel a slow pulsing, a disc-shaped energy moving and stretching me under my eyes, through my cheeks, extending through the back of my head. There is also a rapid pulsing, like a round ball around my chest, pumping in and then relaxing out. Sparkle Lake is vivid and wide, larger than the physical area of my pelvis. My feet are two boulders. There are rainbows in all of my cells, every single one. I just gave in to the urge to laugh out loud. I see an arrow shooting through the center of the circle at my third eye. The tip of the arrow is lodged in a lower part of my brain, at the base of my skull. A direct link has been formed. Now there is a caveman standing before me, yanking the arrow out forcefully. I am unaffected by this. He is dancing away with the arrow in his teeth. I say, Go on! I am aware of a hole where the arrow had been, a tunnel through which light and air can travel. I can see out of that third eye. And the base of my brain where the tip had been is buzzing. Damage? Awakening. Reorganization. It feels heavy there, full in a new way. The rest of my body is still full of white light and rainbows.

Go in peace.

I feel that I have more questions, especially about the relationship between Universal Wisdom and Time. But I understand that I need to end now and just experience this new way of being. Many Thanks. Bless-ed Be. Welcome God, Active and Aware. White Light of Mercy. Heaven and Earth, Unify in this Presence.

Go In Peace.

Go in peace.

Anything else?

Be One with this. Be Love.

I experienced a huge learning curve following that experience. I started out on this book project by just, well, writing a book. I committed to an idea that I didn't know that much about. The topic is a little unusual. I never considered the idea, however, that writing the book would change me. Imagine that. Not only am I growing as I go, but I also understand that I am being groomed, or trained, as I go. There is more to come, and I must be prepared and able to do the work. I have to develop. It's somewhat frightening, this big unknown. I fear getting way out in a place I can't get back from. I know that is not true, but there is the fear nonetheless. A big thing happened, maybe just the edge, but there was direct contact with All That Is. It resulted in a reorganization of my energy pathways and my cellular function, palpable movement in my cerebellum. I have been thinking about that change. I sense that this has something to do with equilibrium—how I understand things in relationship to each other and in relationship to me and myself in relationship to me. It's not a loss so much as a shift, a loosening of my attachment to linear time, freeing me up for other movements, psychic travel. I feel it already—the disconnect from everyday life, especially from other people. I assume that there will also be some intense connections with anyone who occupies the same psychic space. Right now, I have a sense of isolation.

So here I am. I feel buzzy right now. Thank you for the connection.
Is there something for today?
Universal Wisdom: *Yes.*
I feel very sleepy. But I also feel this buzzing in most of my body. Is that the Resonance?
Yes.
It is time to listen.
It is time to Be.
Time to Be. I feel sunken into myself, as if my energy body is huge and my awareness is pillowed in it. There is Sparkle Lake, as big as a wading pool below me. I even see the tops of the mountains that

ring it. The sun is brilliant on the surface of the lake. My awareness is somewhere below my eyes, in my brain stem. I could fall asleep. Do I need to be here?

Go into the Dream World.

Sleeping or waking?

They are the same.

So we travel when we sleep?

Certainly.

I keep hearing the name of Carlos Castaneda.

He understood dreaming.

Should I be reading that?

You need to be doing it.

Practicing?

No. Doing it.

Somehow, I think that if I go there, then I will lose the ability to type.

Why do you need to type?

Oh. Well, I was thinking of recording it for the book.

Not everything is for the book.

Yeah. I'm getting that. Personal development is part of the story, but it's not The Story.

It's your story.

And there are many.

Infinite.

In the stories I've been given so far, it's the resonance that counts.

That is when things are moving.

I am just sensing this, too—that I need to be creating resonance myself. Is that correct?

Your actions, whatever they are, contain resonance. It is how they add to the harmonics that is important.

My mind is showing me bridges. I recall the recent information about serving as a bridge.

A bridge has the capacity to combine the resonances of both sides, to hold them simultaneously.

A joining. At first, that sounded like a lot of effort, but the strength of the bridge is in its structure.

And its ability to sway as needed.
I saw myself with a foot in each world and my arms cradling, as if I was holding a baby and rocking it.
You must be a mother to the child that the union creates.

I have told a few close friends about this meditative connection, and they marvel at it. I am uncomfortable with this, because I do not have much ego attachment to the skill. I have moved well into the teaching, and the connection is the method. Is there anyone around me who can comprehend this level of education?
Universal Wisdom: *You have been given a gift. As you use it, you will find the few who also know.*
It feels crazy-making to talk about it with people who don't understand.
How else will you find others?
I keep sensing that there is a group on the horizon, that I am approaching a time when I might connect with this group.
The group is here.
The Teachers?
Yes.
I have often noted that I don't have much energy in the field behind me. As I let the above information settle in—that the Teachers are a group that is already here, I felt the back of my energy field fill in. So the Teachers are a supportive group. When I accept that, I can see endless spirit-people, mostly women, behind me. And now I see an endless group in front of me as well, facing me. They are less defined, bluish-gray shapes, the Future. I am supported by the Teachers and facing the Future. All around me is full of energy bodies. There is a defining line where the Teachers and the Future meet, and that is me. As far as I can tell, I am with the Teachers, in full color and personality. I don't see myself in the crowded future. There is a blue-gray hand waving to me from several rows into the future. I see a shy young girl. She comes through the crowd to the front and approaches me. When she reaches me, she turns around and stands in front of me, facing the future. Her "body,"

her presence, has joined mine. The blue-gray of her face and body extend out from mine. The bodies of the future have turned so that they are not facing me now, but are looking forward with me and the Teachers. And now a compression is occurring, and the Future bodies are joining together and holding hands. And the Teachers behind me are cheering exuberantly. The Future bodies are dancing a folk dance together, and the Teachers are singing a gospel song. I am dancing the dance *and* singing the song.

And now I am standing alone, and there is only the sound of my voice, clear and pure. And typed words are coming out of my mouth, their sentences unfurling like ribbons in the breeze. They are wind chimes tinkling. I am dancing the folk-future steps. Where my feet meet the earth, they thud softly, like a drum, a heartbeat.
Little birds are flying around me. I am on the pow-wow ground and a rainbow is streaming out behind me. I am dancing counter-sunwise, hands on hips. I am smiling.

Now I am back in the physical world, and my young daughter is asking for breakfast. She had been reading quietly while I was typing.

I'm still a little confused about linear and nonlinear. I get it that linear means one thing follows another and nonlinear means it is all occurring simultaneously. There is a quantum physics application—it is what allows multiple dimensions, because they all exist simultaneously. Accepting this destabilizes "reality."
Universal Wisdom: *Yes. And makes movement possible.*
Movement is somehow related to linear vs. nonlinear?
Movement is related to nonlinear. Movement is shifting attention from one location to another.
Are you saying that space is fixed and time is not?
Space is nonrelative. Space is the everything that time exists within.
And location is?
Where your attention rests. You can choose different locations in Space and Time by organizing your mind to rest there.
Obviously, the mind is a tool that humans use very little of.

Yes. This is part of the change that is coming. There will be a shift. And humans will become aware of new dimensions. There will be an upheaval over this, because those who do not understand will be frightened by it. They will want to control it. But the old ways of controlling others will not apply, because this is a silent manifestation. Only those who manifest the shift will understand it and be truly aware. Others will feel left out. They will have difficulty seeing that this new awareness is a choice. A choice to shift attention or not. You are wondering about why some, like yourself, have been "gifted" with this.

Yes.

Everyone has this gift. Not everyone is willing to destabilize in order to use it.

There has to be trust and faith.

And experience.

This is why I was cautioned to be careful about sharing it. It has become clear to me that few people around me are willing to entertain the possibilities.

Or they are not there yet.

A few days ago, I realized that if I had expressed this access as a child, I might have been locked up or medicated as mentally ill. What is to keep that from happening now?

Discernment. Being scrupulous about who you share with.

But then how can the book come out?

Not all of this will be in the first book. People have to be led. First, they need to understand the resonance, learn to feel it. That will make them curious to go further.

That is why the book is small and easy.

They will all be small. There will be a set.

I see them. Each one has a different color binding, making a rainbow.

Don't get too far ahead.

Right. I also think that I will need to protect myself, that there will be people who want access to me personally.

You will author under a pen name.

This is good. I don't want to get ego-ized through this.

No.

What can I hold until I return?
Know that the universe is supporting you. Live with resonance.

There have been many times when the universe supported me in unexpected ways. I have had many opportunities for growth, and not just cognitive, physical-brain, growth. As I delved deeper and deeper into the Unknowing, the energy connections in my mind were reorganized. This required that I allow a destabilization to occur, and the universe supported me in that state until I could establish a new equilibrium.

Another time, as I connected with the Eye of God, I felt that I was being given directions:

It seems like the Unknowing is in my mind. The travel through the dark to the Window of Unknowing could be my own eye, my own mind. As if I am an instrument of God.

Universal Wisdom: *You are an instrument of God, but not in the way you are thinking. In the Unknowing, you are traveling through not-time. When you come to the eye and see, you place yourself in Time.*

What about when the seeing is vision-dream?

That is Unknowing, when things are shown. You are waking up in Unknowing.

You must look into your heart. Ask.

I see a small person waving to me, waving me toward them. Who is there? It is **Healing Grandmother**. She is pointing at the ground. She has stamped her foot lightly to emphasize her pointing. I have been looking at her finger. Now I look at the floor. We are in the clouds, standing, and below through the wisps I can see the earth. I see the green of trees, and I see city buildings. I am standing there and a car pulls up. I go to it. It's a small blue car. One of my sisters is the passenger. She comes to me and opens her mouth. I am swallowed in the blackness.

Here is a beautiful lake now. Someone is paddling a red canoe below me. It is me paddling. I am heading for shore. There is some activity there, people moving around. There is a campfire, benches around. The people are shadows. I enter the clearing where the fire is smoldering. I sit down on a bench, and instantly there are women all around me. An old woman in a blue dress is across from me. She leans on a walking stick, but she has vibrant energy. Other young women are there, quiet. I see my sister. She is talking to me but I cannot hear. She swallows me again. And again I am paddling, and coming to shore where the fire circle is. Every time I look at my sister I travel to the circle.

What if I look at the elder? The elder is motioning for us to come together and to stand up. She is motioning up to the sky with both of her hands outstretched, the stick in one hand. I am looking up at the blue sky, a pale blue, like the color of her dress. Her hands are gnarled. She is looking at me and I am entering her eyes. I am tumbling through the black. There is the white light at the end of a dark tunnel. I am in the mist again. I am an angel, but this time I am spinning and turning. And my hands are green. When I come through the mist, I am at the red-canoe lake. I am flying to the fire circle. The elder is there. I am the smoke dancing up from the fire. I am with the prayers of the women's fire. I look into my heart. The elder is standing there and waving good-bye to me. I am floating up with the smoke. Away, away. High into the sky. I dive down again and drift up with the smoke-prayers. I am to be up here, in the prayers. I am being cleansed. Something is falling away. Grit, like sand, is sprinkling off of me. I feel lighter and cleaner. I am becoming pure, and lighter, bright white. I can no longer see myself, because the light is so bright. I am up high in the clouds. Healing Grandmother is beckoning me with her finger. I go through the window again. She is on the sill with me, her arms outstretched, her hair streaming. I am curled in a ball, like a fetus. There is lightning and rain. She is summoning power. Her face is wet with rain. I am a bundle, turning and turning. My eyes are closed and I am peaceful, sleeping. Here is a tunnel of white clouds. I stretch through, like a baby being born. When I come out, I am very small. Healing Grandmother is very big, and she is holding me in her hands like a newborn, looking down to me with a little tear in her eye. And now she is lifting me up, to offer me to the sky. Down again, to the earth. A rainbow arches above me, in her hands. Now I am wrapped in a pink blanket and put in the cradleboard on her back. It is time to observe. Her walking is rhythmic. I stare at the dream catcher before me, swaying and tinkling with beads. Vaguely, I see the green of the village beyond. There are red lightning bolts coming from the sides of my head, zaps. I can hear Grandmother singing softly, a welcoming song. That is all.

I am still getting used to the change that has occurred, physically. There is nothing uncomfortable about this. I just feel different. Like I am traveling in a dream but have the usual capacity to focus. It almost feels like I've been lifted away from anxiety. I feel calm. I also feel like I am moving through a sea of dreams. I feel ready for more information, to add to the un-building that is occurring.

Universal Wisdom: *You are right. Change is occurring. It is not, however, the change that you are imagining. What is happening is a removal of some brain waves, patterns. This frightens you.*

It does. I witnessed my grandmother in Alzheimer's. After a while all she had was wisps of consciousness, not enough to support life.

Yes. That did happen.

Suddenly, I feel mistrustful. Have I allowed something I shouldn't have? Something feels a little sly. I dreamt last night that I was being led astray by someone sly and interested in using me, supported by another being. I was being trapped. At the last second, I yelled, "No!" and then woke up, feeling disturbed. Who is this I am talking with?

I am sorry you are untrusting.

I feel tangled up. I just read a small Carlos Castaneda excerpt where he is warning the dream apprentice about contact with inorganic beings. I don't feel safe right now. I am going to take a break here.

I get it now. I have to be willing to let go in order to shift. Losing brain-wave connections is only bad if there is no rewiring.

There won't be. That is what the practice is—doing it the new way.
Barriers removed?
Some.
I need to practice experiencing the world in this new way. Maybe I need more patience before I plunge ahead. Asking for too much too fast.
Yes.
I am sorry that I doubted. Some kind of fear crept up on me.
It was too much at once.
I feel pressured. I am starting a new job, and the book is not done. Suddenly, time feels very linear.
But it can be nonlinear. Focus on what is before you, what you are doing right now. Hold all of the space at once, with everything in it, and then take each thing as it presents itself.
I don't have to herd it around.
No. You already know that, but you have a behavior pattern.
I am worried about money, too, and being an adequate parent, being effective at work, letting down my friends.
Those are the same pattern.
It always seems to show up.
Worry keeps you from holding all of the space.
That somehow decreases my anxiety, because I don't have to feel responsible for it all, just aware of each thing. And holding all of the space means that there is a *lot* of space that does not have something in it. All of my little worries and rationalizations are like moths at the flame, but they are not the flame, and the flame is what is important. And the flame is what?
Spiritual home.
There is that overwhelming sense again, huge gratitude related to this expansively good fit. The Resonance. I am creating Spiritual Home. I am currently very focused and clear, without sleepiness. I cannot recreate the resonance just by wanting to, but when I say "spiritual home" it fills me.

The word nonlinear describes something through absence. Is there another way to describe it? Circular? "Hold all of the space at once, with everything in it" — not holding, like clutching, but holding like focusing? Holding my attention. Circular time? Linear time and inclusive time. I'm not getting much help here.

You're getting there.

Spatial time. Spirit time. It's not-time. Timeless space.

Pretty close.

Linear time and timeless space. Spirit space. Spirit dimension. It is another dimension.

Yes.

Collective.

Yes.

Collective Unknowing.

Yes.

Unknowing leaves a lot of space. What we don't know is a lot, a lot more than what we do know. And it's collective because it contains everything?

Not everything. You haven't gotten there yet.

Thank you for being so patient with me today.

My awareness includes not-knowing. That's pretty big.

You are moving.

So that is movement—accessing different dimensions.

Yes.

And that is something to practice—being in the new Collective Unknowing, and moving back and forth. Bridging. As was discussed earlier, with a foot in each world and mothering the child that produces.

You have to learn to live this Unknowing.

It feels like peace of mind.

That's a little loose.

I want it to be loose ... or not?

Not.

I'm confused. I thought one of its benefits was letting go of tight control.

But not all control. Things may want to sneak in there that don't belong to you.

I was about to complain about that. How can I know, when it's about not knowing? But then I see that the stuff I do know has to be my own, not the whole world's. Own my stuff but not everybody else's.
Resonance.
Resonance, yes. Feeling resonance. There is a sense of knowing when right action or right path is being taken. What if someone has not experienced that?
Everyone has.
Some might not remember. Is there a distilled question to ask?
How does this feel?
That implies intuitive knowledge.
It exercises intuition.
Practice brings ease.
Connection strengthened.
Awareness, then discipline, then lifestyle.
Then Life.

-5-

Crossing the Veil

Once I was able to understand not-Time and become more aware of Space, I recognized that Space is where it is possible to cross the veil. The veil is the thin but powerful curtain of perception that separates the "real" world of physicality from the "dream" world of spirituality. Crossing the veil requires that I honor my energy body as it exists in the dimension of Space.

One part of my daily energy practice is to acknowledge "field," the physical boundaries of my energy field. I have always seen that as setting a limit. I could look at my field and it would extend to the horizons in all six directions. And I assumed that this was spreading myself too thin, draining me. I have worked on pulling it in to concentrate myself more.

Lately, with this concentration, my field has become visible. It originates from center and is especially visible when Spirit has filled my entire body. It is a mass of colored "particles." They are multicolored and multidimensional, and they remind me of pixels from a photo, except that they are 3-D and in motion. They are most concentrated at the core, and then they spread out from there, becoming less dense as they move outward. They are not exactly an identifiable mass. They are a floaty mix in constant coordinated movement, like a shoal of fish or a flock of small birds, moving separately together. When I observe my field, its boundary is the outer edge of the range of the spirit particles. The edge is not well-defined, because some particles are beyond it. My outer boundary is merely the edge of the most concentrated density.

Seeing this allows me to understand that acknowledging field is not so much about *setting* a limit as *reaching* it. It's not about keeping energy out. It's about nurturing what is within. Then I can think of elipting—what happens when I allow my emotional energy to become entangled with another's energy (sometimes called co-dependency), and how that misshapes and overreaches the boundary. Maintaining a boundary is about a maintaining a healthy distance for managing my energy. I don't want to restrict *or* dilute my energy. I want to honor it.

I went to a yoga class one night—only my third time. I had really enjoyed it the previous two times. This night, the room was too hot, and I felt too sluggish. Most of the time, I was just wishing we were done. At the end, the instructor has a relaxation period. There was very nice piano music.

I found myself dancing with my spirit body. My spirit body and my physical body were two separate beings. The dance was long and exploratory, and used the entire gym. We danced with each other, at times joining and un-joining in very fluid motion. Interestingly, my spirit body did have eyes. They were a little weird, those disembodied eyes in the school of pixel-fish. At one point in the dancing, we were mirror dancing, where we both did the same thing opposite each other. There was flying and all kinds of beautiful motion. It was very pleasant. The dancing lasted a long, unhurried time. At the end, as I was lying on the yoga mat, my spirit came and lay down in my physical body, matching its body parts to mine. When the coming together was complete, my whole body was tingling, like little bubbles popping all over my skin. Wow. The whole thing was wow.

What I learned from this experience is that "me"— my physical body, and my spirit are not the same thing. The part of me that is not-spirit is my body. The part of Spirit that is not-me is the *experience* of not-body. So these are two different but connected parts of me that have different purposes, different functions, and they work together.

This raises more questions for me. What is the purpose of Spirit? Communication, apparently.

Universal Wisdom: *Yes, communication. Carry and transfer of information through the Zone.*

(Zone describes the infinite dimensions of space.)

Where does it go?

It goes and comes. It is picking up information wherever it goes and sharing information wherever it goes.

It is primarily a transporter.

No. That is how *it works. That is not its purpose.*

And that was one of my questions. What is the purpose of the spirit?

The spirit is connected to other "places," non-physical if you will.

This is so curious to me. I understand that I have responsibilities in the physical realm, responsibilities to take care of this body and have experiences here, but I am also so attracted to these other realms. I keep seeking any other human who is willing to even talk about the existence of these other realms.

You have been gifted with a connection to these other realms. Sometimes you have neglected your physical world by not honoring that connection.

Yes. This is true. I do feel driven to explore these other realms. Today, I am trying to make sense of purpose. How do these realms connect in a meaningful way, and why? Where does my spirit go when it's not in me? What is sleep? Why is communication with these other realms important?

As you know, your spirit is interacting on many planes simultaneously. It "comes back" (it never really "leaves") when you draw attention or consciousness to it.

If it is interacting on other planes at the same time it is in my body, then am I having effects from its interactions elsewhere?

Yes, but humans are usually not tuned in to these vibrations.

And is my spirit interacting with other people's spirits?

Under the best of circumstances, when the person is clear and open to the Zone, there can be some rather direct interaction. It seems that this is what you seek in a relationship. At the same time, spirits are constantly interacting anyway, because that is what they do. But the information exchanged is not specific or personal—it is general. It is part of what informs instinct and intuition. It is another layer.

Is there choice to that?

Yes and no.

This is part of Collective Unconscious?

Yes, that is another area. Just like you have effect in the physical world, that spirit is involved in but cannot act on, because the spirit is non-physical.

For example, if I build something with physical materials, like wood.

Yes. Even though Spirit is in the process and in you and in the wood and in the thing created, it cannot do the building.

Spirit sounds like "essence."

Yes, although essence implies a passive arrangement, which is only partly true.

So there is an active part too.

Yes.

I'm thinking of the maintenance required for my physical body, and wondering what is required for my spirit body.

Good question. The spirit requires a healthy balance too. There needs to be a healthy welcoming body for it to "come home" to. We have discussed that before. There is another aspect, that humans are trying to address through religion. As we have said before, religion has failed to integrate the ego in a balanced way—usually either denying the ego or abusing it through power over others. The balanced ego is one that recognizes its unique abilities on the physical plane and uses them as a vehicle for spiritual development. Spiritual development integrates the information from other realms into the physical plane. The spirit is the medium for that development.

When Ego is balanced and Spirit is active, then Soul Path is streamlined. This is when healing occurs and everyone moves again toward One-ness With All. It is the smoothing out of the circle, the string of light which joins the beginning and the end, manifesting wholeness. Vibration is cleared, allowing direct communication with other realms.

One of the reasons you feel frustrated in your quest is because you have not recognized that this is about more than you. Individual effort is not going to bring you into other realms because the energy pathways in general are not currently clear. This requires that many travel the path. It is the reason why this information needs to get published, to add to the information that already exists, to give more people more ways to get there. It is about humming up, and while it is important to clean your own house of fuzzy energy, it is also your task to help others on this journey. And the "you" is not just the author of this book, but everyone who is reading it.

This is a unique "time" in linear history, where more people are not struggling with basic, everyday, physical survival. The responsibilities of wealth are to use this opportunity to advance energy healing, not through commercialism, but through personal observance and change. There are no bandwagons to join, just personal practice in True Love. True Love requires that you travel in The Zone and recognize others there too.

If I can "allow" my spirit to fill my entire body, where is it when it is not in my body?
Universal Wisdom: *It is home.*
Home. There is a spirit home?
Yes.
Is it a place?
It is not a location in the sense that you are used to thinking about. It is a matter of distribution and concentration. When you bring your spirit into your body, you are concentrating it. When it is not in that shape, it is spread over other energies.
Other dimensions?
Yes and no. Some energies attach to cells in your body. Others spread out to communicate with other spirit particles. Some of those are in other dimensions, as you call them.
Please describe dimensions.
Dimensions are spatial units. These are hard for humans to comprehend because you are so used to everything being defined by Time.

123

Dimensions are nonlinear. It feels good and affirming to have my spirit concentrated in my body. My spirit also appears to be somewhat amazed at the "feeling" of being with my body. What is the typical arrangement between Body and Spirit?

In your culture, Spirit is primarily a behind-the-scenes presence. People are vaguely aware of it, some more than others. Spirit is always available but rarely gets invited.

What is the ideal arrangement?

It is best when Spirit and Body are working together as an energetic team. This means that body has optimal function, and mind is not only aware and open, but welcoming.

So Spirit prefers to work through the physical body?

Spirit is "physical" too— it is just a less-dense presence.

Is sleep important because of Spirit?

Yes. Body cannot travel where Spirit needs to go, so the body "sleeps" while the spirit travels.

It sounds a lot like when the computer goes to sleep. It doesn't stop functioning. It moves into a lower mode.

Yes.

What is the spirit "doing" while it is not concentrated in the body?

It moves in concurrent spaces.

There is a shift in the way is it transfigured.

The spirit is not one thing. It is many things simultaneously. Sometimes your awareness is able to perceive it as a shape or a presence. The spirit is not what you perceive. What you perceive is spirit as you are aware of it.

Are there ways to improve my perception, to "see" more or better?

You can practice meditation. The one-ness comes closer. As long as you are a physical body, you cannot comprehend this.

Right now, I have a sensation like the energy of my cells has exploded, not a violent change but there is more space between everything, even extending out beyond my body several feet.

That is always there and available.

How can this information about Spirit be helpful?

You can keep practicing this. It is possible to enter other spatial units.

With much practice and guidance. What is the benefit of this kind of work?
The benefit is a greater understanding of your place in the Universe. There is much to be done, on many levels.
This sounds like purpose. This is for humans, or for all living things, or …?
This is going on all of the time. In all times. Moving the energy of the universe. It is what we are meant to do.
I wonder if it is appropriate at this time to bring up Soul. What relationship does Soul have to this discussion of Spirit?
Soul is the energy that Spirit is made up of. It is that which needs to be moved, that which Spirit works with.
So Spirit is the form that Soul takes?
Yes. It is the dream which the physical world is made out of.
Spirit is the dream or Soul is the dream?
Soul is the dream. Spirit is the dreamer.
And body is?
Body is not-dream, the vehicle for the dreamer.
There are many ways to look at this. It is important to see that they are all related, they are all important. Good health helps one enjoy the physical world, but it is also important in helping the spirit to move Soul.
Bring Love into this discussion.
Love is the dream that Spirit dreams. Love is the energetic "stuff" of the universe, the basic form, Life Force. As we have talked about before, there is not Hate or Evil, there is only Harmony and Disharmony. There is only Love and Love Hidden.

You have said that Soul is the energy that Spirit is made up of and that Soul is the dream which the physical world is made out of.
Spirit is made up of Soul, and then Spirit expresses Soul as Love in the physical world. Humans function in the physical world and are physical expressions of Spirit—Spirit that is made up of Soul/Love.
These seem to be important distinctions. The spirit is "made up of," meaning that it *is* Love. And the body is "made out of" Spirit, it comes from it.

This is too detailed. It all comes from Love, it is all made out of it. They are just different expressions. The most important thing is to be aware that Love is the basis. We need to cultivate Love and Life Force. We can know it is happening by the sensations and the outcomes. The basic question is: Are you producing Harmony?

I can't help but notice that sometimes you are using the term "we." Who is "we?"

All beings, sentient and nonsentient, all elements of Life, all who are One.

Who is this that is speaking to me?

*It is **Mathilde.***

How do I know you?

You are the one who carries my stories.

We are back to cellular memory.

Which is also Spiritual Memory.

I am honored to carry your stories. I realize that what you are sharing with me is universal story.

That which cannot be lost.

And it is getting lost.

It is getting buried.

And this writing is to bring it to the surface.

It must become part of consciousness again. Humans need to make the effort to reconnect spiritually.

I am losing battery power on my laptop. Will you come again tomorrow?

I never go away. I am only waiting to be asked.

As I thought about moving the energy of the Universe, I began to wonder about my close relationships with other people.

Can someone talk to me about intimacy?

Well, that would be me.

(I see a young black woman with beautiful, round rosy cheeks and an infectious smile.)

I could talk to you about that, because I am always working on that myself. This is something that people ought to know about, but they don't. Usually, they don't even want to ask about it. It's scary to a lot of folks. Like, getting all naked with yourself or anybody else will make you unlikable. Because then you would see everything that's not right about them. They would see it themselves, or someone else would see it. That is really too bad. Because it would be just as likely that someone would see what is right about you, what's good.

We can be so judgmental, you know. What is it that makes us so ready to judge? Well, it comes from not trusting, not trusting that we really do know what is good or right. We get all messed up by messages around us. Yes, some of those messages are Christian—that everyone is unclean, a sinner, and the only way to be good is to be in heaven, so you can't possibly be that on Earth. That has gotten so twisted up. Because what was really meant there was that you can always do better. Once you have consciousness, like Eve and Adam did, then you have choices to make. And you can choose well or not. Hating yourself and others is not a good choice. If you believe that only Jesus can make a person clean, then you'd better make sure that you know what you mean by "Jesus." The real Jesus is about Loving, and that has nothing to do with judging or excluding. It has to do with opening, not shutting down. It's about Loving.

Whatever way you are living, you need to be asking yourself: is what I am doing really opening up my heart? The hearts of others? All others? Am I letting my spirit communicate with other spirits? It's not all about talking. There is so much that can be done using energy. Your spirit wants to communicate with others. It wants to interact and harmonize. That helps your spirit stay fresh and energized. If you are not doing that, then it finds some other way to do it. Spirit leaves, you know, to find those connections. Yes, some stays behind to keep things running, but it doesn't stay home much. You got to make home a welcoming place to be. Home's got to be a place where you can have varied experiences—meet people, touch people, witness Nature, laugh and smile. Enjoyment feeds Spirit. But a lot of people get this mixed up with comfort and pleasure. Those things are fine too, but they are not a substitute for Harmony.

Harmony is about making connections. The kind of connections that come back to you later with enjoyable memories. Not the fleeting pursuit of pleasure, but the long-vibrating tones of enjoyment. You can look at a sunrise and say, "My, that is beautiful." And you can look at a sunrise and get that feeling like all is right with the world. They are different experiences. You can't manufacture enjoyment—it's something that you feel, something that feeds you. It's not quantity but quality. It's what happens to your insides when you experience it. It's what happens to your spirit. Does it harmonize your Soul Path? When you are living that kind of life, you will be attracting other spirits, because they will be able to sense your spirit's energy.

You do have to be a little careful, because some of the spirits that are attracted are those that don't have a good place to go home to. They are very hungry and wanting to attach. Spirits with a healthy home will want to touch and connect, but they also want to go home again. If you really want to help those hungry spirits, then you will need to help the person make a healthy spirit-home for themselves. Yes, I hear you thinking about the spirit house that you made for your family.[10] That was a good start. You may want to think about building on that. For your family, choose some times to light up the house and talk about what is in there, how it is harmonizing or not.

For yourself, you want to ask your spirit every day: what do you need today? Practice increasing the frequency of checking in. It needs to become second nature. Yes, you have been doing that when you need to make a decision. It works well, doesn't it? People call that using your intuition. But think about doing it in the absence of a requirement (like making a decision). Choose some other reminder, like on the hour, or every time you go to the bathroom (hopefully, a quiet private moment), or upon waking or going to bed. Let your spirit know that you are interested in paying attention to it and to what feeds it, what helps create harmony, what helps it feel at home.

---

10 Regarding the comment, above, about the Spirit House: I went through an emotionally brutal end to my marriage while my children were still very young. While mourning the loss of our family, I was directed to create a Spirit House, a tabletop home for the spirit of our family. I made a small box out of cardboard and decorated it with stones and birch bark. On the inside walls of the little home-made house, I glued dozens of words that represented the core of our family values— Love, patience, humor, respect, etc. My children helped. We placed a small candle inside the house and lit it to reignite the spirit of our family.

Practice feeling your spirit in your body. Your practice of welcoming your spirit into your body every morning is a good start. Add to that. When you are checking in with your spirit during the day, welcome it into your body and notice whether it comes in or how far. Ask what would help it at this time. See what adjustments you can make. Notice when your spirit is in or gone, or only partially in. Check not only your surroundings, but your reaction to them. Are you making room for Spirit? You could ask: what would it be like if there was just a little more room for my spirit here? This is the essence of grounded-ness, of centering. It's about being "all there," which is really all Here, present. Being present means Spirit is present. Spirit will not be present in a situation that is home-less.

I hear you asking about the cellular memory level. When the spirit in each cell hums up, then the body can hum up. They are interconnected. Someone else talked about that before—spirit being present in each cell and in the entire body. That is where the energy pixels came from—an aggregate shaped by multitudes of individual cell energies. Proximity to another body assists communication. Healthy communication between bodies refreshes cellular energy. That is intimacy.

I hear you asking about people without partners, how you can accomplish this. Meet people, touch people, witness Nature, witness Spirit, laugh and smile. It is okay to accept touch. You are thinking about massage. You are right—this is limited, but that does not mean it does not have value. Change your expectations and choose your body worker carefully. Body workers are careful to avoid sensuality. But they should not avoid Loving. It is a difficult balance and the practitioner needs to be skilled. Ask people you trust to touch you.

I have been feeling guilty for being hurt by a single friend who recently partnered.

There are two parts to that. You are envious of something that you think you want. And you have lost a connection with your friend, one that you enjoyed.

People come and go. I know this. What about this intimacy that I think I want? Am I deluding myself?

You are not deluding yourself. You think that you want this. Most of what you can imagine is what it would feel like to be energized again. Long-term relationships are difficult to sustain because constantly

129

sharing energy with another one gets to be the same over time. It can lose its refresh value. People need to know this and work with it, not just expect the connection to stay high-level. Maintenance is a reality.

Today on my walk, I asked if I was being too picky. I was told that I wasn't, but that I needed more patience. I have also asked to be led to a partner. (I changed my tune from asking for them to be sent to me.) Today on top of Eagle Mountain, I asked to be led in Love, to have guidance and support in walking a path of Love. This feels like the opening that is discussed above. Also, making my body a Spirit Home. I really don't think that I am ready for the kind of relationship that I envision.

No one is. So much of it is on-the-job training.

Just like parenting.

Just like parenting. It is important to choose wisely. For these connections to work, the other needs to also be aware of Spirit.

And power dynamics and energy maintenance.

This is a good start. Take a break now and digest.

Thank you so much. Can I ask who this is?

*I am **A'Riquea.***

You have a very gentle tone. I appreciate that. Thank you, A'Riquea.

Is there more to hear about intimacy?

A'Riquea: *There is always more. But sometimes you can be overloaded. So we aren't going to say much more right now. There is something you should know about when you are practicing opening to Spirit, Spirit coming into your body. Sometimes when you do this kind of work, you will get pulled off of other areas of your life. Some other things will be unattended while you focus in the new area. You may experience some confusion, or strong feelings, or bodily discomfort. You can't always change that, because you are working on a new skill, but try to listen to those things. Use them as reminders to come back and take care. It would be possible, for example, to assume that your spirit is your body. It is not. When your body is calling you, it means you are not attending to it. Make sure that you are paying attention to balance. For a while, you may feel like you are tipping back and forth between extremes, until more integration occurs.*

I have a question about caffeine use.

Any kind of stimulant can help you generate more energy. Actually, to generate the sensation of more energy, but whatever energy is created by caffeine is borrowed from somewhere else. You will have to pay it back at a later date with lower energy. The only true way to generate more energy is to hum up, actually tune up the orchestra. This requires rest and exercise and spiritual growth. That is a process, not an acceleration. Like anything, stimulants can be used in moderation, but not as a substitute for true spiritual connection.

Okay. I'm also thinking about returning to online dating.

You find this entertaining. But it is a removed pathway, not a connection. It is entertaining because it is safe. There is no harm if you spend just a little time there. You have other work to do. Don't let yourself get distracted.

I could also use some hints for the coming holidays. I have many family and community obligations. It is easy to see how I am going to be pulled off of self-direction again. Any pointers?

Use this opportunity to expand socially. Try to make connections. You had a good idea to initiate conversations by offering some personal information along the lines of what you would like to hear from the other person.

Go-First.

Yes. Look at your patterns, too, and see if there is a way to make them less routine. Mix things up a little. Have some fun! And pull back from work. You can't accomplish everything at once. Choose something to work on and go slow. Find ways to get out of your office, don't be alone in there. Get out. About your family—lower your expectations, for yourself and them. Go low key.

This is an amazing amount of guidance. Thank you so much for the support.

It is in everyone's best interests.

That is interesting. I help others when I take care of my own business.

When you clear your channels. You do have a gift. It helps us all when you use it.

I can see how it helps me, of course. I also get it that clearing my energy creates healing in many directions, in many dimensions. Explain how it helps you.

It makes it possible to communicate important ways of seeing things. Universal.

(The words are getting fuzzy. There is something here that is not translatable.)

It can be translated, but it includes sensation and awareness. Words do not describe all of that.

Right now I feel connected to other dimensions, but not in a way that I can describe.

You are on the edge of coming through.

I can feel it when I close my eyes, a change in density, especially during my out-breath. When I breathe in, I am more in Time. When I breathe out, my energy simultaneously collapses and expands. I don't want to breathe in, but of course I have to. I am trying to maintain the same density change through both in and out breath. ... I can't sustain this. Too new. I sense a lot of people on the other side. A'Riquea is right there. They are all looking at me hopefully. What will happen when I can manage this change?

Nothing that you can understand right now.

Of course. I see this now. It is part of the arrangement, leading me to be able to move across.

Stories from across the veil.

Yes. I am a little frightened. Sometimes people go and they don't come back?

That is a scare tactic to keep people focused on maintaining the dimension of Time. Some people do not want to give up what they think of as stability. We are here to support you. Because we want to be able to communicate more, we will be assisting you as you transition. It is true that you cannot come back the same way, because awareness changes your perceptions. Your world will be richer. It will be more important than ever, however, to find other people you can connect with—who understand crossing the veil.

I wonder how I will find these others.

Keep practicing going out to socialize. Use the Go-First technique. You will know right away who hears you. Do not get discouraged by the scarcity of connections. Each one will be deep.

Something is changed in me now. I feel a different vibration. Low-toned. Almost a heaviness.

This transition is incomplete. To return, focus on your physical surroundings.

I want to go to the other side. I know I am not ready. What can I do to prepare?

You are a good student. Your curiosity will keep you engaged.

Okay, I have to admit that I am also experiencing a little bit of a creepy feeling, like I am getting primed for *Rosemary's Baby* or something.

That is the instability. Take your time. Take a break.

Thank you. I am quite blown away.

Go talk to someone. Increase your physical awareness. Eat something flavorful. Massage your body. Smell a strong smell. Let go. Don't hurry back.

Okay.

I was blown away by that journey to the edge of the veil. It is exciting to think that the opportunity exists and is coming. I am also afraid of it—scared by the idea that I am not skilled enough to go *and* get back. Oh, I hear the solution—I still have my body, which will retain energy and Spirit to pull me back into the physical world if needed. Okay, then my next fear is that I will get tangled up with negative energies, that this could somehow be harmful.

Universal Wisdom: *It's not. It is for the greater good.*

I want to believe that.

You won't be able to go until you are ready. You can't get there without a certain skill level.

I've been wondering, too, if these fears somehow parallel my social fears in the human world, that there is some danger in making myself vulnerable, even though that is the very thing I long for.

Do not confuse vulnerability with intimacy. You do need to be vulnerable to be intimate, but just because you make yourself vulnerable does not

133

mean that you are being intimate. Intimacy is a condition between two. You have been vulnerable and then abused in that state, so of course you are wary of vulnerability. You have more skills now for protecting yourself. Maybe too many. You have missed some opportunities for intimacy because you were busy leaving instead of looking.

I have noticed that lately—I want to get up and go when I feel closed in.

It is good to be noticing. That is the beginning of change.

I checked in with my spirit today, and was surprised to find that Spirit is who wanted to get up and go.

Spirit is newly invited in your world. Spirit is reacting to the energy of anxiety that you generate.

I could ask Spirit to stay and help me when I feel that anxiety.

That is not Spirit's job. You need to make Home a welcoming place. That means managing your anxiety and relaxing. Practice sticking around and discovering the safety of most situations. You will make some mistakes, but they won't be major.

How can I keep moving forward in my work community?

You can't. You will need to work outward. You need to spread in many directions. You are doing well with positive regard for others. It is noticed. The next thing is to be dangerous.

Dangerous?!

It will be hard for you to do, but you must go where you think you are not welcome.

Like when I went to my first sweat lodge, and I went even though I was afraid of being out of place?

Not exactly. There you weren't sure if you were welcome, so you checked it out. It was fine. This will be something else. You will have to step into the fire of a difficult situation. You must stand calmly in the fire and remain centered. You can do this. You have done it before. It is something that is placed before you as a test.

I remember once when I was walking on a beach, and one my Rasta friends led me into a hidden test of my centering. I was walking with my friend and a man came out of the bushes at me, screaming and ranting right up into my face. When my only response was to raise my eyebrows, the "crazy" man totally relaxed and smiled, nodding his head in approval to my friend.

That was very mild. This will be bigger.

I see myself in darkness, having a big snarly reaction.

That is what is expected of you. That is not who you are. You are wiser than that. You will appear calm and accepting.

There is a big difference between passion of the ego and passion of the spirit. Ego would be reactive. Spirit would be Loving.

Passionate Spirit would be moving, moving toward the other spirit in compassion. Ego shields itself—passion makes it selfish and defensive. Spirit is compassionate, it takes the other in and provides comfort in the face of aggression. You already know this. You will pass the test.

If this is known, than why have the test?

It will make your compassion visible. It will also provide awareness for others on their paths. This is not about you. It is about the interaction. It will be a learning opportunity.

There are so many layers to come ...

I have been thinking a lot about Spirit and about going across the veil. I find myself bringing some of the teaching topics into regular conversation—being naked with where I am. I am trying to think of a good Go-First opener, without being too immediately intense. What do I want people to know about me? That I am very interested in spiritual topics, that I want to hear what other people are thinking or learning. So I have to say what I am thinking and learning. I could say that I am writing a book—that gets people's attention. When I tell them what it is about, they will either be there or not. That would be a good lead into what they are experiencing. I'm a little uncomfortable with the book lead, however, because for most people it attracts ego (status, etc.), and that is not my intent. I could say that I'm doing research for a book, and ask what spiritual topics are current for them. That's a little less direct. I will try that. Any other ideas?

Universal Wisdom: *You could say that you are interested in how people's spiritual experiences influence their everyday lives. Of course, you will have to be ready to answer that question yourself.*

It influences how I spend my time, with whom, and where. It's pretty much the most important thing in my life. It is the undercurrent of everything, even my job. That's a lucky place to be in.

More about choice than luck.

Other people make other choices.

Everyone is making choices all of the time. But do those choices feed or diminish Spirit?

I have been considering that these last few days. I had assumed that Spirit is just something that is always here. I didn't understand how much responsibility I have to create a home for Spirit or how important that is. Spirit is made up of Soul, which is made of Love. It's important to make a place for that. When I typed the previous two sentences, I could feel my body fill with Spirit. Energy density increased. Say it again: Spirit is made up of Soul, which is made of Love. It feels like I am settling into more layers. Soul is made of Love. Love. Each time I type it, I settle into one more layer. If I go back to Love, that is where I am going to cross the veil.

Yes.

I feel the settling of Love, and that is the collapsing portion of the energy shift. Last time I experienced the energy shift, there were two parts: simultaneous collapsing and exploding. So, there is simultaneously a settling deeper and deeper and there is also expansion. It feels like reaching out to an energy field boundary. What else is there?

Letting go.

Un-attaching.

Yes.

Settling and letting go. Collapsing and expanding. Centering and letting go. Love and let go. Going both directions at the same time. Somewhere in the space between is the crossing of the veil.

(I stop to practice this.)

I can see and feel the energy shift in front of me, but not yet all around me. It has to include my entire field, surrounding me. There is a sensation that goes with this—heavy and light at the same time.

Let the sensation guide you, even though you will have to leave it behind to actually travel.

I am suddenly moved to tears that this information is being shared with me. I feel so honored, so grateful, so humble.

That is part of the movement too. As you enter the Face of God, you will be exposed to intense radiance.

This is what I feel when I am Touched by God?

Briefly. When you actually cross, you will be functioning within that Grace.

I see "people," beings on the other side, who are in a kind of library, lining up their information and getting ready to transfer it.

There is much to send back with you, but you will not be able to tolerate very much at first. Yes, they do know that you are preparing. Do not focus on them. They will be right there when you appear. For now, you will need to keep preparing for the journeys. Yes, you have heard right—that means being rested and clear. It means taking care of the body with as much attention as you give to your spiritual life, listening and making time. It means consistent attention to the influence of the ego. It means constantly making choices that nourish the process. Go-First interaction is important too because it keeps even your social interaction focused on Spirit.

I am practicing the energy alignment. Love and Let Go. There is a man in a library, holding up a sheaf of papers. I want to go there. It is interesting to see the process. Before, I was swallowed by the Other. This time, I see the Other being swallowed by me.

It depends which side of the veil you are on.

Should I swallow him?

See what happens.

He is in my mouth, but cannot go down. I feel the edges of his body and his papers in my mouth. When I Love, he settles to my belly. When I Let Go, his hands use my arms to hold out the sheaf of papers. He is clearing his throat to read. He looks something like Albert Einstein, and now that is the appearance of my body too. He is wearing a rumpled dark suit and his white hair is wild. Now he will speak through me:

Library Man: *This is what I have to say: All of the Universe is made of one thing.*

(I am trying to interject what I think, and he is telling me to let go of my mind.)

All of the Universe comes together in one place. There is one place, one space, outside of Time. This place is the space between Energy Points. Energy Points are concentrations of Light. They evidence on human radar as energy. Energy is made of light, not the other way around. Energy Points are concentrations of Light that are visible to sensation. There is more Light than this, but we are unable to detect it. If we are to work with what we know, then we need to understand Energy Points:

Light accumulates there through a process of transformation. The process is dependent on direction. Light is directed by choice, it moves in response to Choice. Choice either moves Light into an Energy Point or away from it. When enough Light is concentrated in an Energy Point, it can communicate with Light in other Energy Points. Any Light that is moved away from Energy Points exists in the space between the points. This is also the space through which Energy Communication occurs.

The Universe exists in the Points, but it is most active in the space between Points. There is much more space between Points than there is occupied by the Points. Communication, therefore, occurs in the Zone of Traveling Light, a multidimensional sea. Light that is fixed in an Energy Point is not static. It is moving in and out of the Energy Points continuously. All of the Light is being shared.

Humans are efforting to maintain the Points in a static arrangement. What they need to be focusing on is the space between points, the Zone of Traveling Light. That is where this information is coming from. Humans need to see themselves as part of the Zone, not just made up of Points. Humans are made of Points. Each cell is a Point. But each cell is made up of smaller Points with Zone between them. And a body is made up of cells with zone between them. Being "In the Zone" is not just a cute phrase. It describes what can occur when Humans are paying attention to the Sea of Movement between Points. Being in the Sea/in the Zone, means that you can tap into the Potentials of the Universe.

Potentials are not held in concentrations like the Points, they are held in the Zone around and between the points.

This Zone is also referred to as the Unknowing, the Great Mystery, and other terms like this. It is the Letting Go portion of Universal Energy. Love is in all Light. It is concentrated in the Points. It is too brilliant to look at. There has been too much focus on Points and not enough on Zone. The time is coming when evolution will require ability in the Zone.

Just now, I was losing contact and needed to practice Love and Let Go. Doing Love and doing Let Go, two things at the same time, requires energy control. It can be tiring. Doing Love and Let Go as just one thing energizes both the Points and the Zone. At the moment, I can only manage this in the close boundary of my own energy field. I imagine that more will happen when I can expand that boundary. For now, I am just practicing Love And Let Go as a single technique.

I think that this is all of the energy shifting I can manage today. The Library Man is protesting that there is more. But I also need to digest this. I cannot promote this material unless I understand it and practice it. I need to integrate before I go to the next level. Thank you.

I meet with the Library Man again on another day. He tries to tell me his name. It is something French, but I cannot hear. (This often happens when they are speaking a language I do not know—I can see their mouths move but I can't hear the words.)

To start, I will enter the Zone. When I Love And Let Go, I feel my energy move to my core (my spine) and also to the edge of my field. There is then a "zone" between core and field, through which the information passes. It is like making space. It is not totally empty, but it is certainly less dense.

I have to mention that sometimes when I am doing this, I feel the nagging doubt of personality, that this could not possibly be real and I must be making it all up. To that, I must say, "Yes, that may be true, *and* it is also true that this is happening. No need to decide. Just do it." That returns me to faith and support.

I am in the Zone. I see the man at the library table with his sheaf of papers. I open my mouth and the man walks in. He stands on my tongue, and when I swallow, he falls smoothly headfirst down my throat. My hands are his hands. He is surveying the papers, deciding where to start.

Library Man: *This is difficult now, because there was momentum before. We are a little lost at the moment. We were talking about Points, and the Zone between them. How energy is made of Light, and Light is made of Love. Yes, yes. It is important to understand these arrangements.*

This is the key to Universal Balance—that Love continue to move through the Zone. Love is the foundation. You can call it other things, like Life Force, or Radiance. The name is not as important as what it does. When Love moves, then everything is touched by the vibration of its light. It keeps the hum going, the vibration that brings everything into alignment. Of course, vibration occurs within a range, so there is a constant exchange between Harmony and Disharmony, and alignment is not permanent.

I am seeing a string from an instrument, plucked and vibrating.

Yes. There is Harmony on any given string, which is the same as a DNA strand. There is also Harmony between strings, and between beings made up of strings. The Harmony is evidenced in the Zone. Harmony allows communication. Communication allows Balance. There is not just one note. There are many all at once. There is a different note to each situation.

Choice, or direction, determines the level of Harmony. When the Zone is humming, then all of the Points related to it (and that would-be all Points, because the Zone is continuous between Points) receive renewed energy, because Light is moving in and out at a vibrational rate. This is a critical point: Enriching the Zone enriches the Points, and both the Zone and the Points are enriched through the movement of energy, which is Light, which is Love.

It is also important to note that there is not a finite amount of Love. More can be created all the time. You have seen this, when a baby is born and more Love is created. Love cannot be destroyed. It can be ignored or denied, and then the Zone loses some vibrancy. The quality of the Zone in any one area is affected by the Points most immediate to it. Zone quality will dissipate over time, but before it does it provides feedback to the nearby Points.

The Points will want to choose a response that increases Life Force whenever possible. Sometimes the bath of negative Zone makes it very difficult to choose more Love. But this is what must happen if balance is going to occur. We, on this side of the veil, are interested in motivating humans to choose more Love, for themselves as evolving beings, and also for us, who share the Zone of Traveling Light/Sea of Movement in some dimensions.

It is important for humans to make Choices in Love. That does not include righteousness, indignation, my-way-or-the-highway thinking. It involves listening, and choosing well for all, choosing from a spiritual connection. Religion must be set aside. Religion does affect cultural conditioning, but not conscience. This was discussed before: is your choice producing Harmony? That is the bottom line. Harmony, not to be confused with safety for the ego, is a quality that resonates to the core. The core functions best when it is connected to body, mind, and heart. The core is the energy collapsed to Love, the Spirit.

This is dense. I think I need to take a break. Is there anything else before I go?

There is one thing that I wish you would tell your friends.

Which friends?

Your spiritual friends. Tell them that there is One Place in the Universe, and it is the Sea of Movement. Everyone needs to practice, every day, creating Love in the Sea of Movement. That is all.

Could I please ask your name? It helps when I come back.

My name is not something important. You may call me just by thinking of me. I will know.

Thank you very much.

Au revoir.

I have been inviting my spirit into my body and my being every morning and also checking in during the day. I have a definite sense of where it is. I understand that it is up to me to make a home for Spirit. It is not going to persevere and push me along—I have to make room for it through appropriate choices. I'm not clear, however, on the relationship between Spirit and "me." What is the "me," and how do we interact?

Universal Wisdom: *The thing that is called "me" is a complex interaction of energies. Yes, we have talked before about the positions of Ego, Spirit, and Soul. They are really not such separate things. They interact and inform each other. They are all related. Yes, you are remembering that Spirit is the fuel. Spirit is what takes the energy and creates more energy. It is a magnifier. But it also must be fed energy. Yes, Ego takes the energy and turns it into action. Spirit takes the light and turns it into energy.*

I am experiencing an internal clash. At the beginning of this conversation, I swallowed the Library Man. Then I decided I wanted to talk with my spine, so I moved back to Universal Wisdom. The Library Man is very adamant, however, that he needs to speak.

Library Man: *This is critical to understanding. You see Spirit as a kind of energy mass in motion. Yes, much like a school of fish—there are separate fish, but they act in concert. They are a unit. You see them as multicolored because they are light prisms. They take light and express it as energy. Somehow, there has been a mistake in understanding, that somehow light is a form of energy. Something has gotten reversed. Because it is really about taking light and making it into energy. That is what makes the spirit fish able to move as one—there is communication in the space between fish, in the Sea of Movement.*

Yes, of course, that is the next question—what is the spirit made of? What are those "fish?" If we could look closely, we would see that each one is a star in the universe. It is too bright to look at, but inside each star is another universe of galaxies and stars. And each person, that is made up of stars, is a star themselves. It is infinite in both directions. Yes, of course, so you are asking about the relationship between the person-star and the cellular-stars. (That's what the fish are, after all—cellular.)

This is all about communication in the Sea of Movement, the Zone of Traveling Light. For energy to continue to be produced, there has to be communication. In order for there to be communication, there has to be awareness of the Sea. Yes, it does happen on its own. That is what survival mode is, where the energy takes over and maintains the lowest level just to keep going. That is a good observation—that death occurs when one no longer inhabits the Sea of Movement. In death, the energy is all pulled back and the organization/organism dissolves. Then the components of each cell go on to become part of something else.

As we were saying, the organism is capable of survival mode, for some period of time. This is not good maintenance. This is like running your car without ever changing the oil or adding brake fluid or filling your tires. People are also making poor choices, like eating fake food and watching TV, and that is like putting the wrong fuel in. There are going to be breakdowns. You are seeing that with the massive decline in health of the general population. Western medicine has gone off on the wrong track, looking for treatments to help these people pretend they are not making bad choices. Western culture has gotten fixated on treating symptoms. No one wants to be responsible for their own mess. Yes, this is where we get back to Spirit, because attention to Spirit will lead to better choices.

Of course, people will want to know how to get there, how to focus their attention. They want someone to tell them—this is the same outside-fix mentality. It has to come from within, because that is where Spirit is. This is where the return to feminine energy comes in. People are afraid to focus inwardly. They are not used to it. They have been taught that the head is the place to look for enlightenment, and they have even been taught that the body is a source of evil. The body is the home of the spirit. It must be treated with respect and honor. The interior needs to be welcoming and alive. It cannot be cut off and denied. Spirit also inhabits the mind, but not the mind exclusively. There must be full integration for the mind to contribute in a positive way. This will sound like a tall order to most people—take care of the body and take care of the spirit. But they go together. One is not possible without the other. Once people begin to be awake to the spirit, they will understand this.

I hear you asking about religious spirituality.

(They can read my mind. I do not have to ask the questions. They just know the question as soon as I think it.)

It is possible to reach spiritual awareness through religion, of any kind. Of course, true spirituality transcends religion. So anyone who uses their religion to say that they are spiritually evolved or superior is going to be stuck on the ego level, and not be the clear spirit that they claim to be.

Recall that the spirit is made of Love, and that is where the Light comes from. True spiritual activity requires movement in the Zone of Traveling Light. That means that Love must be in motion in order to serve the Soul Path. When one is stuck in religious doctrine, it is difficult to keep Love in motion. Recall that the Sea of Movement is interconnected on multiple dimensions. That is what the One With All is. The Love has to be able to move to any other location in the Sea, not restricted by who has the mightiest grasp on a Point. It is about Zone, not Point. It's not that Point is unimportant, but humans have neglected the Zone. There is not enough balance.

Yes, this is correct: Point can be aligned with "masculine" and Zone can be aligned with "feminine." Obviously, this is not the same as male and female. Masculine and feminine describe different ways of focusing energy—knowing and unknowing, concrete and mystery, physical and dream. The current focus on the body has been in service to itself, not in service to spirit. Body needs to serve Spirit. This is about balance. Not stasis, because that is impossible, but balance. Are you creating Harmony?

Now I have heard you asking, "Where does the Light come from? What is it made of?" This is something that is very difficult to place in any concept that humans would be aware of. Yes, Light comes from the Face of God. To say that there is a starting point or an ending point is impossible. Radiance is something that connects multidimensionality. Yes, you are struggling with words, because they don't necessarily apply here. I sense how persistent you are here in trying to understand this.

I am being shown the blackness of space with a few stars in the distance and an intensely brilliant path of white light. I am entering the path. It is beyond hurricane force. I am tumbling and battered. The flow is pushing me at a speed beyond comprehension. I am traveling in an infinite arc of Light. My eyes have burned out. My body has burned to nothing. Once I am nothing, the beam is like gel, slow motion. Even sounds are like a record player at absolute minimum speed. I see an embryo floating in the gel-Light. The unformed eye of the embryo has turned and is looking at me. A pupil opens and I, who am now only awareness, am swallowed into it. The pupil opens and closes like a camera lens. I don't actually go through the pupil, I am at the opening. Each click of the lens shows another scene. There is a summer yard party in the grass. Now there is a snow-laden forest in the shade of dusk. If I try to go in, the pupil clicks closed to hold me out. I don't know why, but I keep trying to go through, each time taking on a bodily form and getting caught in the closing lens. I can see on the other side, and it is the black of space, with distant stars floating in it. The little scenes I observed are floating nearby in some kind of frame, each in a separate frame. I can be on the other side, and when I look back I see the back of the Eye. It is flat, like a giant stage flat, bigger than a football field, and golden colored with spots like a leopard. Each spot on the leopard is another eye that I can enter. Every eye I go through leads me to higher multiples of more eye choices. It is infinite, and I am getting smaller and smaller as the eye choices get more and more numerous. There is an orange floating through the air, and it hits me in the forehead between the eyes. The orange smashes open, and the two halves float away like butterflies dancing together. They leave a trail of juice and section pieces and seeds floating lazily in space. I can see the little spritzes of smell, little white balls, as they float along and bump into my nose, all in slow motion. When I breathe them into my nose, I see them enter through pores in a membrane, into the Zone inside my body. The Zone is continuous—outside and inside my body. The little spritzes of smell touch Points inside my body and excite them. It is like a little happy party. I am smiling. I laugh out loud. The energy of my laugh creates a ripple of communication through the Zone. I sense enjoyment in my body. The butterfly orange halves smile, and the seeds and juice dance in space. It is all related. We Are All Related. We are related through the Oneness. I sense that negative experience/toxins can enter my body, too, through the same continuous Zone. When they make contact, Points inside my body shut down. This also shuts down energy in the Zone outside my body. We All Are One.

The discussion of Point and Zone is not just an abstraction. These concepts have very real applications in everyday life:
I woke up one morning thinking about the energy arrangement that I create when I am practicing on both sides of the veil. I can go there pretty easily now. I noticed that it does not include the sense of being Touched by God, and I realized that it's not about receiving energy. It's about *moving* it. The Sea of *Movement*, the Zone of *Traveling* Light. I see now that this is a major part of aikido—moving energy. And that must be what yoga is too. General movement must be a good start, a way to practice, but I am imagining that there is more to learn about the qualities of the energy and the movement. Is there someone to comment on this?
Universal Wisdom: *Yes, but you are tiring. It is okay to have low energy today. You need to claim some space for yourself. Quit putting out so much for others.*
Yes, I am aware of that. In my current life, I am stressing and putting my energy into the future, all of the tasks that need to get done in too little time, hyper-organizing to cope with that. And it leaves little energy in the present.
Take a deep breath. Every breath is a moment. Every breath is a movement. Put your attention on your breath without controlling it. No, it is not totally passive. Observing is passive. Placing your attention is active. It is both of those things.
You are wondering about sitting meditation and breath. This is a way to practice finding the Zone. It is an attempt to be freed of the past and the future, to be present in the moment of the breath. It is also to be present in the movement *of the breath. One way to add quality to the breath is to smile on the out-breath. I breathe in, I breathe out and smile.*

We need to be connected to Spirit in order to travel in the Zone. We are given clues when we are becoming disconnected, and one of those clues is emotional pain:

I have experienced so many layers and layers of loss. Opening to the grief, I feel the pain like a knife in my heart. It is something that moves inward. It tears and crushes and bloodies as it goes in. What is the spiritual effect of emotional trauma? The feelings magnify to such an intensity that they overshadow connection with ... what?

Universal Wisdom: Life Force. Remember that Life Force is the positive direction—growth, Love. Emotional trauma has the effect of reducing the energy field. It makes the field narrow. It eliminates the perception of Space. It blocks it out by triggering a survival reaction in Ego. In the face of trauma, Ego shuts out as much of the environment as possible, to limit how much it has to deal with. Without connection to Space, to Zone, energy collapses. It becomes Point only.

This explains so many things: Why I feel the need to sob and wail in my grieving—long exhalations help move me off of Point and back into some connection with Zone. Why carrying pain (mine or that of my ancestors) inhibits spiritual growth—it limits connection with Life Force by stagnating energy in Points. Gratefulness balances pain by drawing attention to Space. And releasing pain is important because it makes room for more Space, makes room for the movement of energy.

Acknowledge your losses. Then re-center and place them in the context of your gifts.

Fear is another clue that we are becoming disconnected:

A friend of mine knowingly created a great deal of damage in my family's life. Afterward, she avoided me because she was afraid to look at what she'd done. Much later, I had a vivid teaching dream about this incident. In the dream, I repeatedly asked this woman, "Where does the fear go?" She kept avoiding me, hiding in a corner under a quilt.

Where *does* fear go? I feel an outward movement of energy when I ask that, a kind of emptying. Where does the fear go?

Universal Wisdom: *Home. Fear is about losing. Losing touch, losing contact.*

With Spirit?

With spirit's home.

The physical body?

The body and the Home.

I sense that there is more than the body.

There is also a sensation. A place you know, where Spirit has contact with God.

And that is in the body?

It includes the body. The body is the sense organ that provides it.

I feel I am in Point and Zone right now.

Good. That is the context. There is no Point without the context of Zone. They interrelate.

A resonance that feeds itself?

It does not feed itself. The interaction creates a harmonic. When the vibrations harmonize, there is a space between the notes. That space is the Void, made evident, God made visible. Fear occurs when the Void is obscured, not felt. Ironically, the fear can add to the obscurity, the dissonance. When fear is reduced, the harmonics can reappear.

Back to the question then—where does the fear go?

It goes back into the Void, the One, the All.

Is it true then that creating harmonics can reduce fear?

Not necessarily. Harmonics would be difficult to produce in the presence of fear. We are back to letting go, which is a result of a change in focus. You can practice this: building a fear, and then shifting attention to a connection in nature, with Zone. You will feel the fear reduce, or dissolve.

Where does the fear come from?

The sense that disconnection is occurring. Fear, itself, is not a bad thing. It can be a tool. The realization of fear is, literally, a call to attention— pay attention to what is happening and shift your attention. Not away from it, but towards something else. Fear is a notice that disconnect is occurring. It is a reminder to reconnect. To reconnect, not with Ego, but with Spirit. You have asked before about courage, which is a good example of balance. Courage is Ego placed in service to Spirit, to move ahead—not blindly, just because it preserves pride—but because it is the right thing to do.

I have heard that courage is not the absence of fear. It is the knowledge that something else is more important.

Exactly.

I am trying to consider what creates fear. A threat?

A threat to physical survival. That is why fear is a tool. Because it is a request for action. Fight or flight are reactions by the ego. A more reasonable action would be to slow down and consider the context of the threat.

I keep running my own scenario, which, in the past, has been social fear (anxiety)—that somehow I will not fit in, will not connect, will be rejected.

Substituting culture for Spirit.

I have experienced this repeatedly, and the fear of social isolation is very real. Isolation can be damaging to survival.

True. But you are mistaking fear of isolation for true isolation. You have used that fear like a shield and turned away contact with it.

And if I was using it as a tool, I would look deeper and settle into spiritual connection.

Reseat yourself in center.

The One With All.

The Original Seed, the Great Mystery. All fears are made within yourself. As is your Home, your spiritual center.

Sometimes our inability to create a physical home for Spirit can create blocks in our energy flow:

Universal Wisdom: *Physical movement, especially regular and aerobic (what humans call exercise), is critical for making the Spirit Home. The spirit is on a higher energy plane than the physical body. For Spirit to integrate with Body, there needs to be a common zone of energy activity. Exercise brings the body closer to the energy level of the spirit. It improves communication on the cellular level, which is also where Spirit connects.*

Yes, I hear you wondering about cellular versus whole-body spirit. That has been discussed before. When cell-spirits are communicating well and humming, then the body-spirit is in tune, and that creates the environment for zone-traveling spirit to hum up too, to dance. They are all made up of the same Light and interrelated. You are correct that your cells need calories and your body needs activity. You also need to allow yourself to have your losses, so you can move through them. Don't store them up as if they don't exist. They are still there and they block movement.

That is the trouble with denial as a coping skill.

Yes, you can only hold things off for so long before they create energy clots, energy blocks. This goes against the drive to movement. Life Force moves around blocks. Flow is inhibited. Sometimes Life Force has to break a block. This is painful but necessary.

This is when "negative" events occur?

Some of them. We do not want to get so focused on cause and effect consequences that we lose sight of the primary purpose, which is Movement, the movement of certain qualities of energy. It is about movement of Light. Remember that Light comes from Love. Reach Out is an example of moving Light on a personal and a global scale.

I've seen this quote several times and I always puzzle over it: "The soul is projection, represent it." Projection of what? I keep thinking back to the metaphor of the train—that Ego is the engine, Spirit is the fuel, Soul is the track. Soul is the path. When Ego is fueled by Spirit, there is a reaction of perfection that shoots the train down the track, down the path. They are all parts of a whole—the engine, the fuel, the track. They exist separately but have no purpose without putting them together into a whole. Is there someone who can talk to me about the track/path/soul?

The Soul is complex. You see it as a track because that is what your mind has projected—a linear arrangement. It works in some respects, because there is some kind of movement, but it isn't necessarily movement from point A to point B. The movement describes more of a field. As if that path could be traversed at a high rate of speed, in a direction with

no discernible beginning or end, and then it would just Be. Yes, like
a vibration. Yes, we are back to Love. Spirit is Love, Life Force. Soul
is the movement of Life Force, of Love. It is a movement that makes
vibrational changes in other energy beings. Soul is projection, of Life
Force. Represent it. Re-present it. Gather it up and present it again.

The word represent is from the Latin *repraesentare*, literally "to show
back" —to be present and then to show that to others. (Remember,
'you must be *present* to win!')

Connecting with others through the sharing of Life Force is an
action that involves energy. It can be nonverbal:

I feel powerful lately, like I am superwoman in disguise. Superheroes
usually save the day. What is the purpose of my superwoman?
Universal Wisdom: *She is one who is connected to the earth, and*
able to embody the strength of Life Force. People will seek her out. Her
vibration is a homing device for those needing strength. She does not
have to seek them out, and she does not have to give her strength away.
Her skill will be in helping others discover their own Life Force. You
have the Midas touch, through your heart.
I feel a settling in my hips and an expansiveness in the rest of my
torso. Almost like coming on to a drug.
You must be careful to not use your power like a drug. Keep your ego
out of this. Yes, expand your field—that is what you are feeling now.
People who enter that field will feel it. An important separation will be
to help them understand that it is not you personally who generates this.
You are Life Force, and so are they.
Will these be verbal conversations?
Possibly, but many will be through other planes, like your recent experience
caring for a person who had attempted suicide. Sometimes the other person
will not even know where it came from or be able to identify it, but their
Spirit will register your energy and respond. Many people in these times
are disconnected from that kind of energy. They do not have others around

them who embody it. But their Spirits do not forget. Spirits are always ready to connect. Yes, that is an important distinction. This is not about giving and receiving. This is about expanding and connecting.
I get this. It doesn't seem difficult. Are there dangers?
Eventually, you will get to a place where you will be able to see more of what is happening in others' fields. You will need more training for that. For now, it is just expanding and connecting.
The word superwoman has too much baggage. I need some other name.
You need no name. Just be aware of the action: Settle, expand, connect. Yes, visuals are good. If you see them, use them.
I have felt less effective in oversoul conversation lately.
You are letting the other do all of the talking. Oversoul communication is a way for you to speak your mind, get your point across. Don't be afraid to use that. Do not make yourself invisible. Visibility is key.

Someone I am connected to has a long history of silencing his feelings and then attacking others when he can no longer tolerate his discomfort. Chronically exposed to this passive-aggressive behavior, I have difficulty controlling my reactions. I become angry and defensive. And then I am irritated with myself for my own poor behavior. What is it that has allowed me to continue this?
Universal Wisdom: *It has hooked into your old baggage, too.*
Yes, and this is something I have trouble admitting. It is easy to blame him.
There are parts of it that are his. And it is okay to call him on that. But it is also important to own your part of it. Model the behavior you expect of the other person.
I have to think about what that would look like. My part of it is … not letting go. So I never approach it from a neutral zone. *Aha!*—and there is Zone.

If I was in the Zone, then I would function better. It would not be so important to defend or protect myself. Personality is what gets hurt, what reacts, what carries the old baggage like a shield. It's worth understanding my baggage but also understanding that it doesn't have an impact in the Zone. And Zone would also be part of harmonious alignment. Comments, please.

We were talking another time about the importance of personal spirit. It is not something you know with your mind. It is something you feel. There is no faking it. In any moment, you are connected or you are not. Spirit wants to be connected, that is part of its purpose. Sometimes it will take the opportunity of an unexpected opening, like a loss or a trauma or intense beauty, to jump in. In those circumstances, people may make major spiritual shifts. To be "born again" is really just reconnecting. As you are aware, depression is about the loss of connection, when the body is lost from spirit. Gratitude increases connection. Love is all about connection, especially Love, the Love that is Life Force.

You are wondering about the relationship between Spirit and Zone. We have discussed this before, and it would be good to go back and look at that. Spirit is present in many dimensions. We are primarily aware of it in the physical realm, because that is where our senses are focused. The Zone includes many more realms than just the physical. That is why it feels so expansive. Spirit functions best when it is relating to those dimensions. Not exclusively, but in addition to the physical realm. The better connected the person is to Spirit and to Zone, the more information is available to them. It comes through the Zone. It is like cells, which need the environment of a blood supply to live. The Zone is the blood supply. It is in constant motion and in constant communication and relationship with other parts of the blood, and all parts of the body, and also the outside environment (air and food), which is connected to the universe. It is all connected. And the cell itself is a maze of connections that go the other, micro, direction. Infinite in all directions.

It is possible for the cell, for a person, to see themselves as only themselves, unrelated to anything else, but that is a very limited perspective. The rest of it is all happening, all the time, whether you see it or believe it or not. The Zone is a place to access it all. The Zone exists both inside and outside the body. It is continuous. When one does not recognize the Zone, then you are stuck in the Point of personality. In that place, there are limited resources. Healing energy is not available in helpful amounts, and the organism deteriorates. The spirit is always there, however, until physical death occurs. So there is not a time when it is not ready to step in. It is never hopeless.

You are asking about the connection between Zone and Soul. We have primarily discussed Spirit because this is something that is personal and accessible. Soul is a bigger perspective. Soul is something that is made up of all the dimensions that Spirit travels in. We have discussed soul path as the track that the ego/engine travels on when it is fueled by Spirit. Soul Path is realized when alignment occurs, alignment with Life Force. These concepts are not beyond the mind of humans, but they are not readily distilled into words that are easy to comprehend. This is advanced work. The first points are to recognize Spirit, create a home for spirit in Life, and get comfortable functioning in the Zone. It is important to practice this and become skilled. This is the foundation for further work. Grandmother Dreams *is the context for supporting this first practice. It is realizing and accepting that which is beyond the physical realm, and practicing the ability to expand there. Across the veil.*

That is all. Now it is time to manifest this in the physical world. Focus on these tasks.

Thank you. I can hardly believe the gifts here.

You accepted commitment to this project. These gifts are the fruit of your own willingness. The purpose of this project is to help people see that the gifts are available to all.

-6-

The Next Direction

As I was readying this book for publication, I was given several experiences that demonstrated the ongoing nature of this work. The first one was a preview of the next phase of the journey. Through this, I began to better understand energy outside of this physical dimension. I met the radiance of God and left my body behind, experiencing the free energy of my spirit. It happened in the following way:

I awoke one morning from a dream where I was having a conversation with a Buddhist Holy Man. For several days after that, His Holiness was in my daily visions, motioning for me to continue or stop what I was doing, directing me. At one point, he asked me to type. I was nervous. He is a person of great centering, and at the time, I felt loose and low-energy. I plunged ahead anyway, because it was the right thing to do.

With great respect and honor, I welcome your presence and assistance.

His Holiness: *You have been preparing for this journey, and now is a time to rest. Your hard work and focus will come to fruition, but not at this time. Yes, you feel disappointed, because you thought you were close to the ending of your project. But there is another experience to have before you can do this. You must come and enter into the golden light.*

I am on a narrow stone-paved street, and he is waving me through a wooden door into a hallway.

I have passed through the door. The hallway appeared dark inside, but now that I am in it, there is a brilliant light, too bright to look at. Intense. I am being Touched by God. I am not centered in my body, however, and do not have the full sensation. His Holiness continues to usher me into the light. I have been standing before it, and now it is clear that I must enter it. There is a buzzing, a static, quite loud, like the sound between radio stations, and I hear someone speaking in an Asian language. I continue inward. It is molten. I am somehow unable to go farther than a frontal sensation. I am holding back. What is keeping me here? What fear? I move halfway in. Now my cells are opening. Each one is a bursting supernova. Still limited to a frontal sensation, I try to turn to expose my back. I feel a oneness with the light, its brilliance spreading through me and outward, extending through my arms and my face. I am a conduit for the energy of God, a source of the radiance, a golden glow of brilliance, a beacon and a healer. I feel the radiance at my back, scouring those cells and making them shine. All over, I am covered with golden diamonds of light. Inside of me is still darkness. Then I see my outer cells making connections, one by one by one, networking the golden light toward my interior. I am rotating in many directions, including upside down. I am in a bubble, close to the center of a huge explosion of light, tumbling in the blast. The connecting is still going on inside my body until all is connected, all is golden, and there is a glowing golden egg of energy at my *hara*, my center. I breathe into it and become one mass of molten gold, encased in the skin of golden diamonds. My mind is multicolored, with blue and red strings woven in it, a giant cloud much larger than my head. I am a creature of Space, surrounded by the green light of Harmony. Suddenly I burst, and glittering diamonds are spread out all over the green field. The molten gold of my body is expanding forth in golden strings of energy, weaving themselves through space as they travel outward. The ends of the strings are red-tipped and red-streaked. All around me are rainbows of sound and light, a cacophony of intensity. My body is now clear, completely transparent, and at one with all that is around me. The cloud of energy that is my mind remains.

And there is His Holiness again. I am outside the doorway and he has his palms pressed together in front of his face, bowing and saying good-bye. I am in the world, in a field of grass and flowers, and here is my body. All of it is like a dream. I want to be back in the rainbow realm, that transparent state. His Holiness is signaling no, that is closed now. I have traveled into a nonphysical dimension and back. He is nodding yes and playfully shooing me away—that is all for now. I feel refreshed from my visit but also disjointed at my return. He indicates the importance of breath. I can come back to this room, even though I don't really want to. I am grateful for this journey, however, this trip into the next chapter of spiritual travel. He nods his head yes—I have been given a sneak preview. This makes me smile, and he claps his hands together joyfully.

Thank you so much! This is a great gift. Namaste.

Namaste. He smiles.

I smile.

I will go eat and walk and be awed by the wonderfulness of Life.

His Holiness came to me again the next day. He led me to a conversation that helped me sharpen my focus on my spiritual purpose. This speaks not just to me but to everyone, everyone reading this. Once we have placed Ego in service to Spirit, we must learn to travel in the Zone and connect with others who travel there. We must not only make a spiritual path, but wear it smooth with use.

His Holiness motions me through the same wooden doorway with shadows on the other side. I see a lot of small figures working on individual projects, something like Santa's workshop, but each figure is floating on a cloud.

You must go to your station.

I look around. I see myself ahead, dressed as I am today and leaning over a table. The little-figure-me looks up and sees the me-who-came-through-the-door standing here. She smiles and waves me over. I look over her shoulder and see that she has a map spread out on the table. She is studying the map with enthusiastic intent, as if the map itself is a great treasure. I ask her, What are you looking for?

I am looking for the way to go next, and there are so many possibilities.
I am looking at the map now too. Around the upper left edge there
is water, and green land with hills marked topographically. For some
reason, I think that this looks like Galway, Ireland.
Yes, I have already been there.
What did you do there?
I found myself in community.
Where else have you been?
I went to Africa, and found myself on this planet.
And where are you going next?
*I am heading out into the Universe. I don't think it is on this map,
however. I have been looking and looking. I don't think that it is here.*
Is there some way I can help?
*I don't know. It is all a big journey. You never really know where you will
end up. But I have a sense of the way to go. I do need your help to get there.
I need you to pay attention to the sign posts—look for the white bears that
came to you, look at the direction they are facing. They know where this
place is that I am going. I will be able to find it if you help me.*
Trusting the Universe.
*That is part of it, of course, trusting the Universe. But there also needs
to be some kind of action that propels us forward. Choosing, to be sure,
making right choices, but also seeking opportunities. You cannot just wait
for something to come to you. Things will come, no doubt, but that is a
very passive arrangement, and then you will have to settle for whatever
happens to drift by. Yes, strategic placement can help that, can affect what
flows by. But there is also this active looking to attend to, the energy of
curiosity that takes you to the next place and the next place. And not just
the next place but the next person. This is something that we have been
avoiding—trusting others. Life has seemed so far like a series of closing
doors. That is one side of that coin. It is time now to actively seek others.
Help yourself relax by not worrying so much about trusting them—trust
in the experiences that interaction creates. Enrich your life with more
human interaction, deeper connections than you have had before. Go
further in your relationships. I know it sounds scary. But this is the next
skill to develop, because this is what we need to go out into the Universe.
This is the way. Right now we need to connect with deeper psyches.*

Opening the channels for more and more travel across the veil.

Yes. This opening needs to be made, and it is through interpersonal connections.

This is what I was told about the book being a vehicle for deeper travel, that moving the book and talking about it is the higher function of the project.

Not necessarily the higher function, but one of the functions.

It would help me to have a clearer picture of my role. Not that I need a label, but a general directive.

This has been discussed before. Your role is that of activist. You are to affect overall relationships toward the greater good. In this case, it is the evolution of human consciousness.

Kind of like a psychic activist?

Kind of. That is a pop culture term. This is more serious.

Spiritual Activist?

Closer. But the words are not as important as the intent, conviction, and action. At this point, action *is what we need. It is time to start moving.*

I have to say that I have been thinking recently about whom I could start a conversation with. Someone came to mind, just because he seems so intense and in the Zone. I have seen him look at me from a distance with a question about connection. There is someone else, who is socially labeled as mentally ill, but I have always connected with him, too, far beyond the physical realm. Are there some guidelines here?

All you can do is ask them.

What I want to ask is how they feel when they are in that deep groove—is it like being in the Zone.

That is a good start. And it's also important to recognize boundaries— yours and theirs—and maintain them. Do not get tangled in their business, just work toward opening the channel and clearing it. It doesn't matter who you are working with. There are many levels—describing the channel, pointing it out, exploring it, traveling through it. You can go with someone, but do not take them there. You do not have those skills yet.

It's interesting that many sports players will understand what it is like to be "in the Zone," when the players all click at once and the sum of their effort is magically greater than all of the parts added together. Musicians will know "the groove," when an energy climax is surpassed and the resulting music is perfect and effortless. I am curious to ask my son about where his energy is when he zeroes in on the hunt to make good kill. There are so many applications right in front of me that I never really considered. Look at all of the body workers and alternative healers I know who regularly practice beyond the five senses. There is plenty to start with.

Yes. There is no reason to go slow here. Make it the focus of your new life.

I feel hesitant, of course, to make myself vulnerable, but also excited to get started on something meaningful. I do have a question: I am curious about who I am talking to right now. You have shown yourself as me, and I am wondering what part of me this is.

I am the part of you that brings the rain and fertilizes the soil. I am the mystery and the passion. I am the un-self. I am your spirit.

Thank you for this journey. Through this work, I now understand the difference between my physical body and my spirit, and the importance of a healthy partnership between them. I have pined for the spiritual realm at the expense of physical maintenance. I now see how important it is to have both a robust spiritual *and* physical presence. They work together and support each other—the fuel and the engine, fine-tuned and traveling the soul path. The goal is to travel this hoop over and over, making it ever smoother, a conduit for Life Force, energizing the planet and the universe, bringing God in closer and closer contact with the human soul.

All Praise for the Infinite Radiance of Love.

Go in Peace.

CPSIA information can be obtained
at www.ICGtesting.com
Printed in the USA
FFOW03n1958121017
41026FF